T0202503

Communications
in Computer and Information Science   1508

More information about this series at https://link.springer.com/bookseries/7899

Maxim Bakaev · In-Young Ko · Michael Mrissa ·
Cesare Pautasso · Abhishek Srivastava (Eds.)

ICWE 2021 Workshops

ICWE 2021 International Workshops
BECS and Invited Papers
Biarritz, France, May 18–21, 2021
Revised Selected Papers

Editors
Maxim Bakaev 🆔
Novosibirsk State Technical University
Novosibirsk, Russia

Michael Mrissa 🆔
InnoRenew CoE
Izola, Slovenia

University of Primorska
Koper, Slovenia

Abhishek Srivastava 🆔
Indian Institute of Technology Indore
Indore, India

In-Young Ko 🆔
Korea Advanced Institute of Science
and Technology
Daejeon, Korea (Republic of)

Cesare Pautasso 🆔
Universita della Svizzera Italiana
Lugano, Switzerland

ISSN 1865-0929   ISSN 1865-0937 (electronic)
Communications in Computer and Information Science
ISBN 978-3-030-92230-6   ISBN 978-3-030-92231-3 (eBook)
https://doi.org/10.1007/978-3-030-92231-3

This Springer imprint is published by the registered company Springer Nature Switzerland AG
The registered company address is: Gewerbestrasse 11, 6330 Cham, Switzerland

Preface

Edge clouds are becoming an important type of computing infrastructure for collecting and processing big data as low-latency and reliable communication technologies such as 5G and Web of Things (WoT) are developed and deployed. Edge clouds are especially useful for efficient and secure data collection and processing for smart cities and smart factories. In edge cloud environments, it is essential to provide Web services for efficiently collecting and processing various types of big data in real-time. In addition, it is necessary to develop a framework for building big data service applications in a reliable and usable manner.

The first International Workshop on Big data-driven Edge Cloud Services (BECS 2021)[1] was held to provide a venue in which scholars and practitioners could share their experiences and present on-going work on providing value-added Web services for users by utilizing big data in edge cloud environments. The workshop was held in conjunction with the 21st International Conference on Web Engineering (ICWE 2021)[2], which was held online during May 18–21, 2021.

The first edition of the BECS workshop focused on the following topics: Web services in edge clouds; Web of Things in edge clouds; AI in edge computing (Edge AI); dependable and highly usable big data platforms; distributed data collection, analysis, and prediction; stream data processing in edge clouds; big knowledge graphs for distributed edge cloud environments; modeling and mashup of edge cloud services; micro-service architecture for edge cloud environments; and edge-cloud interaction and collaboration.

The BECS 2021 workshop started with a keynote talk by Domenico Siracusa who is the head of the RiSING Research Unit at Fondazione Bruno Kessler (FBK) in Italy. The title of the talk was Distributing Intelligence in the Cloud-to-Edge Continuum. In the talk, he explained the need to support fine-grained and dynamic management of resources on the Cloud-to-Edge continuum to deal with the increasing complexity of Internet of Things (IoT) and artificial intelligence applications. He also presented the vision to create and deploy cloud-native applications over heterogeneous and distributed computing environments, and discussed the application of the developed technologies in real-world pilot scenarios stemming from smart city and robotic logistics environments, providing insights on outcomes and open challenges.

In the BECS 2021 workshop, five full papers and one short paper were selected for presentation. The first paper, Putting Data Science Pipelines on the Edge (by Ali Akoglu and Genoveva Vargas-Solar), proposes a composable just-in-time architecture for data science pipelines named JITA-4DS and associated resource management techniques for configuring disaggregated data centers. In the second paper, DNN Model Deployment on Distributed Edges, the authors (Eunho Cho, Juyeon Yoon, Daehyeon Back, Dongman Lee, and Doo-Hwan Bae) analyze the characteristics of split points with representative

---

[1] https://becs.kaist.ac.kr/iwbecs2021/.

[2] https://icwe2021.webengineering.org/.

network configurations that need to be considered to design a proper Deep Neural Network (DNN) slicing scheme concentrating more on actual application requirements. The third paper, Towards Proactive Context-Aware IoT Environments by means of Federated Learning (by Rubén Rentero-Trejo, Daniel Flores-Martín, Jaime Galán-Jiménez, José García-Alonso, Juan Manuel Murillo, and Javier Berrocal), proposes a solution based on federated learning to predict behaviors in different environments and improve users' coexistence with IoT devices, avoiding most manual interactions and making use of mobile devices capabilities. The fourth paper, titled Real-time Deep Learning-based Anomaly Detection Approach for Multivariate Data Streams with Apache Flink by Tae Wook Ha, Jung Mo Kang, and Myoung Ho Kim, presents a real-time deep learning-based anomaly detection approach for multivariate data streams with a stream processing framework, Apache Flink. In the fifth paper, A Novel Approach to Dynamic Pricing for Cloud Computing Through Price Band Prediction, the authors (Dheeraj Rane, Vaishali Chourey, and Ishan Indraniya) define a dynamic pricing model for cloud brokers in which instead of fixed pricing, the brokers can provide a price range to their consumers. Finally, the short paper written by Sinwoong Yun, Dongsun Kim, and Jemin Lee, Learning-based Activation of Energy Harvesting Sensors for Fresh Data Acquisition, defines the estimation error of the sensing data at a measuring point, which increases as the distance to the sensor increases and the age of information (AoI) of the data increases. In addition, the authors define the network coverage, which is defined as the area having the estimation errors lower than a target value.

Although the workshop was held online due to the COVID-19 pandemic, the authors and participants had important discussions on the technical issues relating to the collection and processing of big data in an efficient manner in distributed edge cloud environments.

This book is enriched with two invited papers that are tightly related to the main topic area of the BECS workshop. The first invited paper, Exploiting Triangle Patterns for Heterogeneous Graph Attention Network, was selected from the position papers that were submitted to the BECS workshop. Eunjeong Yi and Min-Soo Kim, the authors of this paper, propose a heterogeneous graph attention network called TP-HAN by which graph patterns can be efficiently exploited from large-scale graphs that are build out of big data. Another paper, Towards Seamless IoT Device-Edge-Cloud Continuum: Software Architecture Options of IoT Devices Revisited, was invited from a related research group. In this paper, the authors (Antero Taivalsaari, Tommi Mikkonen, and Cesare Pautasso) discuss the implications of the IoT device architecture choices in light of the new occurrences and make some new predictions about future directions. In addition, they make a case for isomorphic IoT systems in which development complexity is alleviated with consistent use of technologies across the entire system.

We would like to thank all the Program Committee members and reviewers for their efforts in providing high-quality reviews and constructive comments. Our special thanks also goes to Domenico Siracusa who gave a wonderful keynote talk. The BECS 2021 workshop was supported by the Ministry of Science and ICT (MSIT), South Korea, under the Information Technology Research Center (ITRC) support program (IITP-2021-2020-0-01795) supervised by the Institute of Information and Communications Technology Planning Evaluation (IITP). We are grateful for their support. Last but not least, we would like to thank the authors who submitted and presented their research work for the workshop and all the participants who contributed to make the workshop successful.

October 2021

Maxim Bakaev
In-Young Ko
Michael Mrissa
Cesare Pautasso
Abhishek Srivastava

Organization

Workshop Co-chairs

In-Young Ko   Korea Advanced Institute of Science and Technology, South Korea

Abhishek Srivastava   Indian Institute of Technology Indore, India

Michael Mrissa   InnoRenew CoE and University of Primorska, Slovenia

ICWE 2021 Workshop Co-chairs

Maxim Bakaev   Novosibirsk State Technical University, Russia

Cesare Pautasso   Università della Svizzera italiana, Switzerland

Technical Program Committee

Doo-Hwan Bae   Korea Advanced Institute of Science and Technology, South Korea

Jongmoon Baik   Korea Advanced Institute of Science and Technology, South Korea

Bhaskar Biswas   Indian Institute of Technology BHU (Varanasi), India

Zhipeng Cai   Georgia State University, USA

Javier Espinosa   University of Lyon, France

Chirine Ghedira   University of Lyon, France

Eunkyoung Jee   Korea Advanced Institute of Science and Technology, South Korea

Jeehoon Kang   Korea Advanced Institute of Science and Technology, South Korea

Minsoo Kim   Korea Advanced Institute of Science and Technology, South Korea

Myoung-Ho Kim   Korea Advanced Institute of Science and Technology, South Korea

Jemin Lee   Sungkyunkwan University, South Korea

Faïza Loukil   Université Polytechnique Hauts-de-France, France

Martin Musicante   Universidade Federal do Rio Grande do Norte, Brazil

Placido Souza Neto   Federal Institute of Education, Science and Technology of Rio Grande do Sul, Brazil

Cheyma Ben Njima   University of Sousse, Tunisia
Jongse Park   Korea Advanced Institute of Science and
                                    Technology, South Korea
Kiran K. Pattanaik   Indian Institute of Information Technology and
                                    Management, Gwalior, India
Prabhat K. Upadhyay   Indian Institute of Technology Indore, India
Jules M. Moualeu   University of Witwatersrand, Johannesburg,
                                    South Africa
Genoveva Vargas-Solar   French Council of Scientific Research, France

Contents

BECS Workshop

Putting Data Science Pipelines
on the Edge

Ali Akoglu[1] and Genoveva Vargas-Solar[2(✉)]

[1] ECE, University of Arizona, Tucson, AZ, USA
akoglu@arizona.edu
[2] French Council of Scientific Research (CNRS), LIRIS,
69622 Villeurbanne, France
genoveva.vargas-solar@liris.cnrs.fr

Abstract. This paper proposes a composable "Just in Time Architecture" for Data Science (DS) Pipelines named JITA-4DS and associated resource management techniques for configuring disaggregated data centers (DCs). DCs under our approach are composable based on vertical integration of the application, middleware/operating system, and hardware layers customized dynamically to meet application Service Level Objectives (SLO - application-aware management). Thereby, pipelines utilize a set of flexible building blocks that can be dynamically and automatically assembled and re-assembled to meet the dynamic changes in the workload's SLOs. To assess disaggregated DC's, we study how to model and validate their performance in large-scale settings.

Keywords: Disaggregated data centers · Data science pipelines · Edge computing

1 Introduction

Data infrastructures such as Google, Amazon, eBay, and E-Trade are powered by data centers (DCs) with tens to hundreds of thousands of computers and storage devices running complex software applications. Existing IT architectures are not designed to provide an agile infrastructure to keep up with the rapidly evolving next-generation mobile, big data, and data science pipelines demands. These applications are distinct from the "traditional" enterprise ones because of their size, dynamic behavior, and nonlinear scaling and relatively unpredictable growth as inputs being processed. Thus, they require continuous provisioning and re-provisioning of DC resources [2,4,14] given their dynamic and unpredictable changes in the Service Level Objectives (SLOs) (e.g., availability response time, reliability, energy).

G. Vargas-Solar—Authors list is given in alphabetical order.

M. Bakaev et al. (Eds.): ICWE 2021 Workshops, CCIS 1508, pp. 3–14, 2022.
https://doi.org/10.1007/978-3-030-92231-3_1

This paper targets the execution of data science (DS) pipelines[1] supported by data processing, transmission and sharing across several resources executing greedy processes. Current data science pipelines environments promote high-performance cloud platforms as backend support for completely externalising their execution. These platforms provide various infrastructure services with computing resources such as general-purpose processors (GPP), Graphics Processing Units (GPUs), Field Programmable Gate Arrays (FPGAs) and Tensor Processing Unit (TPU) coupled with platform and software services to design, run and maintain DS pipelines. These one-fits-all solutions impose the complete externalisation of data pipeline tasks that assume (i) reliable and completely available network connection; (ii) can be energy and economically consuming, allocating large scale resources for executing pipelines tasks. However, some tasks can be executed in the edge, and the backend can provide just in time resources to ensure ad-hoc and elastic execution environments.

Our research investigates architectural support, system performance metrics, resource management algorithms, and modeling techniques to enable the design of composable (disaggregated) DCs. The goal is to design an innovative composable "Just in Time Architecture" for configuring DCs for Data Science Pipelines (JITA-4DS) and associated resource management techniques. DCs utilize a set of flexible building blocks that can be dynamically and automatically assembled and re-assembled to meet the dynamic changes in workload's Service Level Objectives (SLO) of current and future DC applications. DCs configured using JITA-4DS provide ad-hoc environments efficiently and effectively meet the continuous changes in data-driven applications or workloads (e.g., data science pipelines). To assess disaggregated DC's, we study how to model and validate their performance in large-scale settings. We rely on novel model-driven resource management heuristics based on metrics that measure a service's value for achieving a balance between competing goals (e.g., completion time and energy consumption). Initially, we propose a hierarchical modeling approach that integrates simulation tools and models.

The remainder of the paper is organised as follows. Section 2 discusses related work identifying certain drawbacks and issues we believe remain open. Section 3 JITA-4DS the just in time edge-based data science pipeline, execution environment proposed in this paper. Section 4 describes preliminary results regarding JITA-4DS. Finally Sect. 5 concludes the paper and discusses future work.

2   Related Work

The work introduced in this paper is related to two types of approaches: (i) disaggregated data centers willing to propose alternatives to one fits all architectures; and (ii) data science pipelines' execution platforms relying on cloud services for running greedy data analytics tasks.

---

[1] A Data Science Pipeline consists of a set of data processing tasks organised as a data flow defining the data dependencies among the tasks and a control flow defining the order in which tasks are executed.

Disaggregated Data Centers. Disaggregation of IT resources has been proposed as an alternative configuration for data centers. Compared to the monolithic server approach, in a disaggregated data center, CPU, memory and storage are separate resource blades interconnected via a network. The critical enabler for the disaggregated data center is the network and management software to create the logical connection of the resources needed by an application [12]. The industry has started to introduce systems that support a limited disaggregation capability. For example, the Synergy system by Hewlett Packard Enterprise (HPE) [3], and the Unified Computing System (UCS) [13] M series servers by Cisco are two commercial examples of composable infrastructures. [12] proposes a disaggregated data center network architecture, with a scheduling algorithm designed for disaggregated computing.

Platforms for custom modelling provide a suite of machine learning tools allowing developers with little experience to train high-quality models. Tools are provided as services by commercial cloud providers that include storage, computing support and environments for training and enacting greedy artificial intelligence (AI) models. The leading vendors providing this kind of platforms are Amazon Sage Maker, Azure ML Services, Google ML Engine and IBM Watson ML Studio.

Machine Learning and Artificial Intelligence Studios give an interactive, visual workspace to build, test, and iterate on analytics models and develop experiments[2]. *Machine learning runtime environments* provide the tools needed for executing machine learning workflows, including data stores, interpreters and runtime services like Spark, Tensorflow and Caffe for executing analytics operations and models. The most prominent studios are, for example, Amazon Machine Learning, Microsoft Artificial Intelligence and Machine Learning Studio, Cloud Auto ML, Data Bricks ML Flow and IBM Watson ML Builder.

Discussion. Machine learning studios address the analytics and data management divide with integrated backends for efficient execution of analytics activities pipelines allocating the necessary infrastructure (CPU, FPGA, GPU, TPU) and platform (Spark, Tensorflow) services. These environments provide resources (CPU, storage and main memory) for executing data science tasks. These tasks are repetitive, process different amounts of data and require storage and computing support. Data science projects have life cycle phases that imply in-house small scale execution environments, and they can evolve into deployment phases where they can touch the cloud and the edge resources. Therefore, they require underlying elastic architectures that can provide resources at different scales. Disaggregated data centers solutions seem promising for them. Our work addresses the challenges implied when coupling disaggregated solutions with data science projects.

---

[2] An experiment consists of data sets that provide data to analytical modules connected to construct an analysis model.

3   JITA-4DS: Just in Time Edge Based Data Science Pipelines Execution

The Just in Time Architecture for Data Science Pipelines (JITA-4DS), illustrated in Fig. 1, is a cross-layer management system that is aware of both the application characteristics and the underlying infrastructures to break the barriers between applications, middleware/operating system, and hardware layers. Vertical integration of these layers is needed for building a customizable Virtual Data Center (VDC) to meet the dynamically changing data science pipelines' requirements such as performance, availability, and energy consumption.

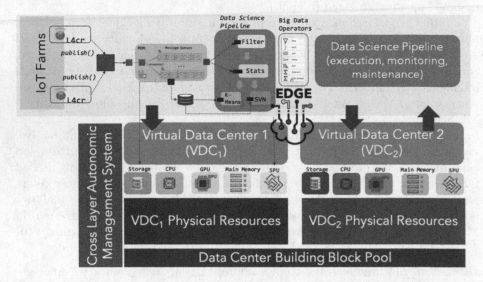

Fig. 1. Just in time architecture for data science pipelines - JITA-4DS

JITA-4DS fully exploits the virtualization from the virtual machine (VM) level into the VDC level (e.g., fine-grain resource monitoring and control capabilities). JITA-4DS can build a VDC that can meet the application SLO, such as execution performance and energy consumption to execute data science pipelines. The selected VDC, then, is mapped to a set of heterogeneous computing nodes such as GPPs, GPUs, TPUs, special-purpose units (SPUs) such as ASICs and FPGAs, along with memory and storage units.

DS pipelines running on top of JITA-4DS VDC's apply sets of big data processing operators to stored data and streams produced by the Internet of Things (IoT) farms (see the upper part of Fig. 1). In the JITA-4DS approach, the tasks composing a data science pipeline are executed by services that implement big data operators. The objective is to execute as just in time edge-based processes (similar to lambda functions), and they interact with the VDC underlying services only when the process to execute needs more resources. This means that services are running on the edge, on processing entities with different computing

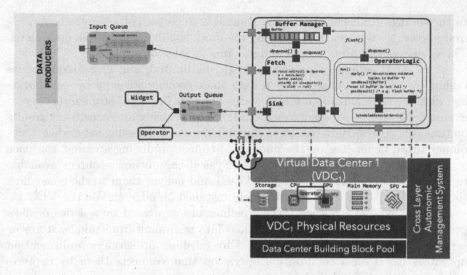

Fig. 2. Architecture of a big data/stream processing service

and storage capacities. They can totally or partially execute their tasks on the edge and/or on the VDC. This, in turn, creates the need for novel resource management approaches in streaming-based data science pipelines. These approaches should support and satisfy the data management strategy and stream exchange model between producers and consumers, invoke tasks with the underlying exchange model constraints on the compute and storage resources in the suitable form and modality and meet multi-objective competing performance goals. Next, we describe the architecture of big data operators, and we show how they interact with the VDC. Later we will introduce our resource management approach for JITA-4DS.

Big Data/Stream producing and processing services. We assume that services that run on the edge produce and process data in batch or as streams. Data and stream processing services implement operators to support the analysis (machine learning, statistics, aggregation, AI) and visualise big data/streams produced in IoT environments. As shown in Fig. 1, data and stream producing services residing on edge rely on underlying message-based communication layers for transmitting them to processing and storage services. These services can reside on edge or a VDC. A data/stream service implements simple or complex analytics big data operations (e.g., fetch, sliding window, average, etc.). Figure 2 shows the general architecture of a streaming service.

The service logic is based on a scheduler that ensures the recurrence rate in which the analytics operation implemented by the service is executed. Stream/data processing is based on unlimited consumption of data ensured by the component Fetch that works if streams are notified by a producer. This specification is contained in the logic of the components OperatorLogic and Fetch. As data is produced, the service fetches and copies the data to an internal buffer. Then, depending on its logic, it applies a processing algorithm and sends the data to the services connected to it. The general architecture of a service is specialized in concrete services implementing the most popular aggregation operations. These services can process data and streams on edge or a VDC.

Since RAM assigned to a service might be limited, and in consequence its buffer, every service implements a data management strategy by collaborating with the communication middleware and with the VDC storage services to exploit buffer space, avoiding losing data, and processing and generating results on time. Big stream/data operators combine stream processing and storage techniques tuned depending on the number of things producing streams, the pace at which they produce them, and the physical computing resources available to process them online (on edge and VDC) and deliver them to the consumers (other services). Stores are distributively installed on edge and on the VDC.

Edge based Data Science (DS) Pipelines are expressed by a series of data processing operations applied to streams/data stemming from things, stores or services. A DS pipeline is implemented by mashing up services implementing operators based on a composition operation that connects them by expressing a data flow (IN/OUT data). Aggregation (min, max, mean) and analytics (k-means, linear regression, CNN) services can be composed with temporal windowing services (landmark, sliding) that receive input data from storage support or a continuous data producer for instance, a thing. The connectors are Fetch, and Sink services that determine the way services exchange data from/to things, storage systems, or other services (on-demand or continuous). Services can be hybrid (edge and VDC) services depending on the number of underlying services (computing, memory, storage) required. To illustrate the use of a JITA-4DS, we introduce next a use case that makes full use of edge and VDC services configured ad-hoc for the analysis requirements.

Use Case: Analysing the connectivity of a connected society. The experiment scenario aims at analyzing the connectivity of the connected society. The data set used was produced in the context of the Neubot project[3]. It consists of network tests (e.g., download/upload speed over HTTP) realized by different users in different locations using an application that measures the network service quality delivered by different Internet connection types[4]. The type of queries implemented as data science pipelines were the following:

```
EVERY 60 seconds compute the max value of download_speed
of the last 3 minutes
FROM  cassandra database neubot series speedtests and streaming
RabbitMQ queue neubotspeed
```

```
EVERY  5 minutes compute the mean of the download_speed
of the last 120 days
FROM  cassandra database neubot series speedtests and streaming
rabbitmq queue neubotspeed
```

---

[3] Neubot is a project on measuring the Internet from the edges by the Nexa Center for Internet and Society at Politecnico di Torino (https://www.neubot.org/).

[4] The Neubot data collection was previously used in the context of the FP7 project S2EUNET.

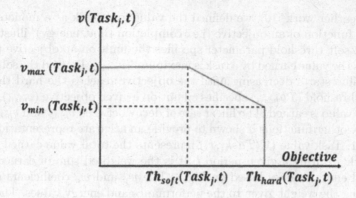

Fig. 3. General formulation for value vs. objective and thresholds.

We built an IoT farm for deploying our experiment and implemented a distributed version of the IoT environment on a clustered version of RabbitMQ. This setting enabled us to address a scaleup setting regarding several data producers (things) deployed on edge. We installed aggregation operators as services distributed on the things and an edged execution environment deployed on servers deployed in different devices. The challenge is to consume streams, create a history of connectivity information, and then combine these voluminous histories with new streams to answer the queries. Depending on the observation window size, the services access the observations stored as post-mortem data sets from stores at the VDC level and connect to online producers currently observing their connections (on edge). For example, the second query observes a window of 10 days size. Our services could deal with histories produced in windows of size 10 days or even 120 days. Such massive histories could be combined with recent streams and produce reasonable response times (order of seconds).

4 Preliminary Experimental Results

4.1 Value of Service Based Scheduling and Resource Management

JITA-4DS encourages a novel resource management methodology that is based on the time-dependent Value of Service (VoS) metric [9] to guide the assignment of resources to each VDC and achieve a balance between goals that usually compete with each other (e.g., completion time and energy consumption). VoS allows considering the relative importance of the competing goals, the submission time of the task (e.g., peak vs non-peak period), or the task's nature as a function of task completion time. A primary difference of our VoS metric from earlier studies on "utility functions" (e.g., [1,5,6]) is the fact that we combine multiple competing objectives and we consider the temporal value of performing resource management at a given instant of time. This ability is crucial for meeting the SLO of edge-based data science pipeline execution, where the nature and amount of the data change dynamically among streams of data arriving from heterogeneous and numerous sets of edge devices.

In our earlier work [10], we defined the value for a task as a monotonically-decreasing function of an objective (i.e., completion time, energy), illustrated in Fig. 3. The soft threshold parameter specifies the limit on an objective (Th_{soft}) until which the value earned by a task is maximum (v_{max}). Beyond the soft threshold, the value starts decreasing until the objective reaches the hard threshold. The hard threshold (Th_{hard}) specifies a limit on a given objective (v_{min}), beyond which zero value is earned. The linear rate of decay between v_{max} and v_{min} can be replaced by other functions if shown to provide an accurate representation.

In Eq. 1, Task value ($V(Task_j, t)$) represents the total value earned by completing task j during a given period t. It is the weighted sum of earned performance and energy values based on Fig. 3. The w_p and w_e coefficients are used for adjusting the weight given to the performance and energy values. The importance factor $\gamma^{(Task_j)}$ expresses the relative importance among tasks. If either the performance function or energy function is 0, then the VoS is 0.

$$V(Task_j, t) = (\gamma^{(Task_j)})(w_p * v_p(Task_j, t) + w_e * v_e(Task_j, t)) \qquad (1)$$

The VoS function, defined by Eq. 2, is the total value gained by n tasks in the workload that are completed during a given time period t.

$$VoS(t) = \sum_{j=1}^{n} V(Task_j, t) \qquad (2)$$

The design of resource management heuristics for the JITA-4DS is a challenging problem. Resources must be interconnected and assigned to VDCs in a way that will maximize the overall system VoS as defined in Eq. 2. Towards this goal, we designed a simulation environment and evaluated various heuristics by experiments for a homogeneous environment much more straightforward than the JITA-4DS design illustrated in Fig. 1. In the simplified environment, we studied the allocation of only homogeneous cores and memories from a fixed set of available resources to VMs, where each VM was for a single dynamically arriving task. Each task was associated with a task type, which has estimated execution time and energy consumption characteristics (through historical information or experiments) for a given number of assigned cores and assigned memory. To predict each application type's execution time and energy consumption, we use statistical and data mining techniques [7–9], which represent the execution time and energy consumption as a function of the VDC resources. As an example, one of the heuristics was Maximum Value-per-Total Resources (Maximum VPTR). Its objective function is "task value earned/total amount of resources allocated," where the total amount of resources (TaR) for a task depends on the task execution time duration (TeD), the percentage of the total number of system cores (Cores) used and the percentage of the total system RAM used:

$$TaR = TeD \times [(\%Cores) + (\%RAM)] \qquad (3)$$

We compare the VPTR (Value Per Total Resources) algorithm with a simple scheduling algorithm applied to a workload that starts during peak usage time.

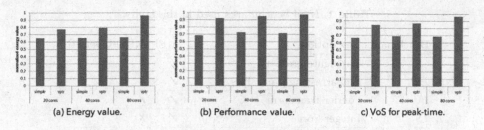

(a) Energy value.   (b) Performance value.   c) VoS for peak-time.

Fig. 4. Value gain comparison of the VPTR over the simple heuristic

For 80 cores, VPTR is able to have an improvement of almost 50% in energy value and 40% in performance value as shown in Figs. 4(a) and 4(b), respectively. Figure 4(c) shows the VoS when we combine both performance and energy values. Because the workload involves a peak system period, the Simple heuristic cannot efficiently utilise the resources, resulting in VPTR having up to 71% increase in normalized VoS.

In general, each of these percentages can be weighted for a given system, depending on factors such as the relative cost of cores and memory or relative demand for cores versus memory among applications in typical workloads. Each time the heuristic is invoked, it considers tasks that have arrived in the system but have not been assigned resources. For each task, independently, for each of its allowable resource configurations that will provide non-zero task value, we find the cores/memory that maximizes the task's VPTR. Then, among all mappable tasks, we select the task with the maximum VPTR, call this task m, and make that assignment of resources to task m, or if the allocation is for a future time, we create a place-holder for task m. We then update the system state information based on this assignment or place-holder and remove task m from the list of mappable tasks.

4.2 JITA-4DS Simulation

Because a composable system is a tightly integrated system, it will create new challenges in modeling application performance and designing resource allocation policies to maximize productivity. This creates the necessity for creating a simulation environment to experiment and evaluate composable systems and use them to design new resource allocation policies. We validated our simulation framework's functionality against emulation-based experiments based on a system composed of 64 nodes. Each compute node is a dual socket with 125 GB of memory and InfiniBand QDR for the network interface. Each socket on the node has a CPU (Ivy Bridge-EP) with twelve cores and a maximum frequency of 2.40 GHz. The TDP of each CPU is 115 W in our system. We access the power-specific registers on each CPU to monitor and control the CPU power consumption. On this system, we collect empirical power-performance profiles for our test applications and create models. We use the publicly available benchmarks from the NAS parallel benchmark suite (NPB) [11]. In our study, a synthetic workload

Table 1. NAS benchmarks used in this study.

Benchmark	Description	MPI	MPI+OpenMP
CG	Conjugate gradient	✓	✗
EP	Embarrassingly parallel	✓	✗
FT	Fourier transform	✓	✗
IS	Integer Sort	✓	✗
MG	Multi-grid	✓	✗
LU	Lower-upper Gauss-Seidel solver	✓	✓
BT	Block tri-diagonal solver	✓	✓
SP	Scalar penta-diagonal solver	✓	✓

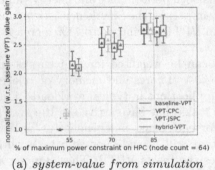 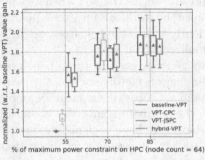

(a) *system-value from simulation*   (b) *system-value from emulation*

Fig. 5. Comparing the simulation and emulation results.

trace is a list of jobs in the order of arrival time. We use the benchmarks listed in Table 1 to form a job in the workload trace. Each job entry in the workload trace consists of job arrival time, job name, maximum job-value, job's input problem size, iteration count, node configuration range, soft threshold, and hard threshold. We experimentally select the sampling range for these parameters to ensure our unconstrained HPC system is oversubscribed. We create offline models for each hybrid benchmark by using the modeling technique discussed in [7].

Similar to our emulation HPC prototype, we simulate a system composed of 64 nodes. We use a similar set of hybrid benchmarks and their models to create workload traces. For the simulation study, we create 50 workload traces, and each trace is composed of 1000 jobs in the order of their arrival time. Each trace simulates a workload of approximately 50 h at three different system-wide power constraints (55%, 70%, and 85%). While simulating a workload trace under a given power constraint, we assume our model prediction error is zero for each benchmark. In Figs. 5(a) and 5(b), we compare the system-value earning distribution from our emulation and simulation studies respectively using a set of value-based heuristics covering Value-Per-Time (baseline-VPT) and its variations [7,8] Common Power Capping (VPT-CPC), Job-Specific Power

Capping (VPT-JSPC), and hybrid that combines VPT-CPC and VPT-JSPC. Even though our power-aware algorithms' normalised system-value earnings are higher in the simulations than the emulations, we observe a similarity in the pattern of the system-value earnings of the algorithms as the power constraint is relaxed from 55% to 85%. The differences in the magnitudes of system-value earnings can be attributed to our simulation study, assuming all the system's CPUs are identical.

Discussion. In the JITA-4DS environment, the resource management problem is much more complex and requires the design of new heuristics. The computing resources allocated to the VDC for a given class of applications are a heterogeneous mixture of different processing devices (different CPUs, different GPUs, different accelerators, etc.) with various execution performance and energy consumption characteristics. They depend on each of the specific applications being executed by that VDC. For example, several aspects remain open, like the ad-hoc design of the JITA-4DS resource management system for a VDC built from a fixed set of components. The design of a JITA-4DS instance is determined by the execution time and energy consumption cost, and resources requirements of a data science pipeline. Therefore, it is necessary to dynamically identify the configuration choices for a given pipeline and define VDC resources' effective resource allocation strategies. In general, for determining the dynamic resources requirements of data science pipelines at runtime, it is necessary to consider two challenges. First, calculate a VDC-wide VoS for a given interval of time, weigh individual values of various instances of pipelines. Second, propose objective functions that can guide heuristics to operate in the large search space of resource configurations. The objective is to derive possible adequate allocations of the shared and fixed VDC resources for several instances of data science pipelines. We have observed that decisions must be made regarding the resource management system for JITA-4DS to divide the shared, fixed resource pool across different VDCs to maximize the overall system-wide VoS. All of the above single VDC challenges still apply and interact across VDCs. Additional problems, such as determining when resources should be reallocated across VDCs and do so in an online fashion, must be addressed. This includes the methodologies for reassigning resources that do not interfere with currently executing applications on different VDCs affected by the changes and measuring and accounting for the overhead of establishing new VDC configurations.

5   Conclusion and Future Work

This paper introduced JITA-4DS, a virtualised architecture that provides a disaggregated data center solution ad-hoc for executing DS pipelines requiring elastic access to resources. DS pipelines process big streams and data coordinating operators implemented by services deployed on edge. Given that operators can implement greedy tasks with computing and storage requirement beyond those residing on edge, they interact with VDC services. We have set the first simulation setting to study resources delivery in JITA-4DS.

We are currently addressing challenges of VDCs management in simpler environments, on cloud resource management heuristics, big data analysis, and data mining for performance prediction. To simulate, evaluate, analyze, and compare different heuristics, we will build simulators for simpler environments and combine open-source simulators for different levels of the JITA-4DS hierarchy.

References

1. Briceno, L.D., et al.: Time utility functions for modeling and evaluating resource allocations in a heterogeneous computing system. In: International Symposium on Parallel and Distributed Processing Workshops and Phd Forum, pp. 7–19, May 2011
2. Chen, H., Zhang, Y., Caramanis, M.C., Coskun, A.K.: EnergyQARE: QoS-aware data center participation in smart grid regulation service reserve provision. ACM Trans. Model. Perform. Eval. Comput. Syst. **4**(1), 1–31 (2019). https://doi.org/10.1145/3243172
3. HPE Synergy. https://www.hpe.com/us/en/integrated-systems/synergy.html
4. Kannan, R.S., Subramanian, L., Raju, A., Ahn, J., Mars, J., Tang, L.: Grand-SLAm: guaranteeing SLAs for jobs in microservices execution frameworks. In: EuroSys 2019. Association for Computing Machinery, New York (2019). https://doi.org/10.1145/3302424.3303958
5. Kargahi, M., Movaghar, A.: Performance optimization based on analytical modeling in a real-time system with constrained time/utility functions. IEEE Trans. Comput. **60**, 1169–1181 (2011)
6. Khemka, B., et al.: Utility maximizing dynamic resource management in an oversubscribed energy-constrained heterogeneous computing system. Sustain. Comput. Inform. Syst. **5**, 14–30 (2015)
7. Kumbhare, N., Akoglu, A., Marathe, A., Hariri, S., Abdulla, G.: Dynamic power management for value-oriented schedulers in power-constrained HPC system. Parallel Comput. **99**, 102686 (2020)
8. Kumbhare, N., Marathe, A., Akoglu, A., Siegel, H.J., Abdulla, G., Hariri, S.: A value-oriented job scheduling approach for power-constrained and oversubscribed HPC systems. IEEE Trans. Parallel Distrib. Syst. **31**(6), 1419–1433 (2020)
9. Kumbhare, N., Tunc, C., Machovec, D., Akoglu, A., Hariri, S., Siegel, H.J.: Value based scheduling for oversubscribed power-constrained homogeneous HPC systems. In: 2017 International Conference on Cloud and Autonomic Computing (ICCAC), pp. 120–130. IEEE (2017)
10. Machovec, D., et al.: Utility-based resource management in an oversubscribed energy-constrained heterogeneous environment executing parallel applications. Parallel Comput. **83**, 48–72 (2019)
11. NAS-NPB. https://www.nas.nasa.gov/publications/npb_problem_sizes.html
12. Papaioannou, A.D., Nejabati, R., Simeonidou, D.: The benefits of a disaggregated data centre: a resource allocation approach. In: 2016 IEEE Global Communications Conference (GLOBECOM), pp. 1–7 (2016). https://doi.org/10.1109/GLOCOM.2016.7842314
13. Unified Computing. http://www.cisco.com/c/en/us/products/servers-unified-computing/index.html
14. Xu, X., Dou, W., Zhang, X., Chen, J.: EnReal: an energy-aware resource allocation method for scientific workflow executions in cloud environment. IEEE Trans. Cloud Comput. **4**(2), 166–179 (2015)

DNN Model Deployment on Distributed Edges

Eunho Cho[✉][iD], Juyeon Yoon, Daehyeon Baek, Dongman Lee,
and Doo-Hwan Bae[iD]

Korea Advanced Institute of Science and Technology (KAIST),
Deajeon, Republic of Korea
{ehcho,bae}@se.kaist.ac.kr, {juyeon.yoon,bdh0404,dlee}@kaist.ac.kr

Abstract. Deep learning-based visual analytic applications have drawn attention by suggesting fruitful combinations with Deep Neural Network (DNN) models and visual data sensors. Because of the high cost of DNN inference, most systems adopt offloading techniques utilizing a high-end cloud. However, tasks that require real-time streaming often suffer from the problem of an imbalanced pipeline due to the limited bandwidth and latency between camera sensors and the cloud. Several DNN slicing approaches show that effectively utilizing the edge computing paradigm effectively lowers the frame drop rate and overall latency, but recent research has primarily focused on building a general framework that only considers a few fixed settings. However, we observed that the optimal split strategy for DNN models can vary significantly based on application requirements. Hence, we focus on the characteristics and explainability of split points derived from various application goals. First, we propose a new simulation framework for flexible software-level configuration, including latency and bandwidth, using dockercompose, and we experiment on a 14-layered Convolutional Neural Network (CNN) model with diverse layer types. We report the results of the total process time and frame drop rate of 50 frames with three different configurations and further discuss recommendations for providing proper decision guidelines on split points, considering the target goals and properties of the CNN layers.

Keywords: DNN partitioning · Distributed edge · Edge computing

1 Introduction

Including visual analytics or augmented/virtual reality, there are various applications for utilizing the edge computing for machine learning. Researchers [2,5] found that there are various benefits for the deployment of machine learning model on edge devices like reducing the time by offloading the processing.

Currently, researches for utilizing the distributed system on machine learning concentrates on orchestration or collaborative schemes among clients, edges, and

---

E. Cho and J. Yoon—These authors contributed equally.

© Springer Nature Switzerland AG 2022
M. Bakaev et al. (Eds.): ICWE 2021 Workshops, CCIS 1508, pp. 15–26, 2022.
https://doi.org/10.1007/978-3-030-92231-3_2

clouds working to create a costly deep learning system. However, there are still many challenges to effectively utilizing ML/DL tasks on edges, such as managing latency and disconnected operation (achieving network transparency), handling heterogeneity of multiple edge devices, and deploying pipelines of (re)training or inference scenarios.

Various studies have suggested frameworks or models that utilizes existing production models and hardware architectures. Although there have been multiple conclusions drawn in research about the DNN deployment framework, such as the early-exit scheme of Distributed Deep Neural Network (DDNN) [5] and production-ready slices [2], there remain limitations that constrain the introduction of DNN slicing on edges in the real world. For example, DDNN requires specially tuned model architecture that cannot be quickly adapted to a realistic environment. Couper claims to generate acceptable quality of DNN slices using general DNN models, but there is space for much more improvement regarding performance. The main limitation of Couper is that we can tune the model and computation power of edges to fit with target application goals. Couper assumes a fixed specification of edge and cloud machines and does not consider the computational ability of the device. Moreover, both previous approaches prematurely generalize the requirements of diverse applications, which can vary significantly.

This paper analyzes the characteristics of split points with representative network configurations that can give us the necessary insight to design a proper DNN slicing scheme concentrating more on actual application requirements. To do so, we first implement a software-configurable DNN inference pipeline on a distributed environment, utilizing Docker and `docker-compose`. Based on the experiment with the simulator, we will provide an analysis of how to find better split points according to the various CNN layers concerning the network environment. Our main contribution is providing a way to determine a more optimized DNN slicing strategy by considering the characteristics of DNN layers and different potential combinations of computational power distribution and network configuration.

The paper is structured as follows. Section 2 describes existing works and the background of our work. The details of our simulation environment are outlined in Sect. 3. Next, the experiment setup and its results are presented in Sects. 4 and 5. Finally, we conclude the paper in Sect. 6.

2   Related Works

Edge cloud orchestrator (ECO) [6] supports federated learning, transfer learning, and staged model deployment by separating the burdens of training and inference. The proposed architecture leverages both edge and cloud by providing an abstraction of the control path. However, their approach still needs to deploy the whole DNN model on a single node, which can burden low-end edge devices in managing large and complex state-of-the-art CNN models.

Model light-weighting techniques presented in the research of Wang et al. [9] and Talagala et al. [6] include other directions that adapt to and specialize in target models to fit with the given environment. By pruning an insignificant portion of the structural part or connection of the models, both the model's size and inference time can be significantly lowered.

However, model compression or pruning techniques have an explicit limitation of reduction to maintain accuracy as acceptable as the original. In contrast, the model partitioning approach that supports deploying each part of the model to the heterogeneous computing environment can benefit the deep learning system on edges and clouds. eSGD [7] supports collaborative training on a CNN model by synchronizing parameters with sparse gradient updating.

One study [1] used specialized, spatially distributed micro-architecture, specifically multiple FPGA chips, for DNN training and inference in a parallel manner.

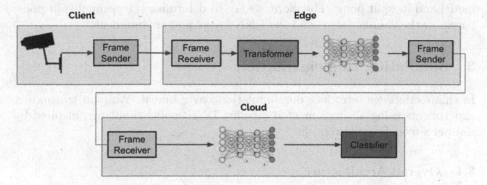

Fig. 1. Structure of the Couper framework for image classification when utilizing edge-cloud environment. [2]

However, at present still, the most practical solution would be to keep the typical hardware architecture and better utilize the existing machines that are distributed geographically. Hsu et al. proposed a solution named *Couper*, which is a framework that creates slices of DNNs and deploys them on the docker-based edge pipelines. *Couper* analyzes the given DNN model and generates the partition for the distributed deployment. To do this, *Couper* supports the automated slicing and deployment on the edge-cloud environment. Figure 1 shows the *Couper* framework on image classification task. On three nodes, client, edge, and cloud, the *Couper* provides the DNN evaluator and two pairs of frame sender and receiver. Another approach by Teerapittayanon et al. [8] proposed distributed deep neural networks that measure the confidence of classification results during the intermediate layers and support an earlier exit of inference, so that more than 60% of the inference tasks could be prematurely completed on edge. In contrast, it still needs a specialized DNN architecture that supports the early exit scheme.

Similar to the architecture of *Couper*, several studies have evaluated the likelihood of the distributed DNN model's deployment on the modern network environment. Ren et al. [4] showed the distributed DNN's deployment on the mobile web with a 5G network based on the distributed DNN model's deployment. This work also shows the adaptive mechanism to figure out the optimal point of partitioning the DNN model. However, this mechanism only depends on the network environment, and so it does not take into account the characteristics of each DNN layer. Lockhart et al. [3] present *Scission*, which automatically determines optimal partitions by layers while considering user-defined constraints about cloud-edge settings. However, it does not support pipelines with multiple edges and does not consider the effect of varying packet sizes and network congestion caused by the different partitioning points.

Although these studies have provided various frameworks for utilizing deep learning on edge machines, there was a lack of discussion on optimizing the framework. Especially for *Couper*, the performance is hardly dedicated to the model and its split point. Therefore, we try to determine the optimal split point based on the various features of the DNN layers and environment.

3 Simulation Implementation

In this section, we introduce our simulation environment. We plan to conduct experiments using an implemented pipeline DNN model simulator, inspired by Couper's model slicing concept.

3.1 Overall Architecture

The architecture uses the latest version of `Tensorflow`, and any model contains the structure of the `tf.Graph` (Tensorflow Graph) could be used as the target model to deploy. Each result tensor produced from the split layer is serialized with ProtoBuffer and `TensorProto` definition provided by a Tensorflow official implementation.

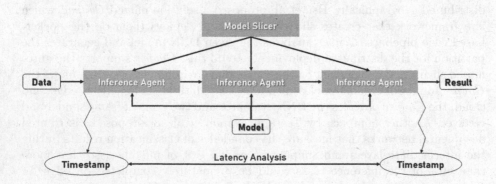

Fig. 2. Overall architecture of the simulation

Figure 2 shows the overall architecture of this implementation. There are two main components. The **Model Slicer** uses the split point as an input and sends the exact target split point to the inference agent. The **Inference Agent** has a full model and split the model by the split point from the model slicer. The inference agent represents a single edge, and each agent has information about the split DNN deployment's pipeline structure. Each inference agent uses a docker with the same container images but a different split DNN model. Based on this architecture, we can analyze based on the frame drop rate probed from the results and conduct a latency analysis based on the total time for processing the specific amount of data.

3.2 Model Slicer

The model slicer initiates every inference agent based on the given split point and pipeline structure. The split point can be based on the operation level or the layer level. The operation level can produce more slices and a better set of slices that is more close to the true optimal. However, many models are complicated and hence contain many layers. In that case, layer-wise slicing can reduce the search time for the split points, and there is no need to discard invalid slices due to the possible branches (this is only present in the operation-level representation of DNN). In this research, we decided to split models by the level of layers. The given split point can consist of a single split point or multiple split points.

3.3 Inference Agent

Our inference pipeline consists of a set of sequential edges that collaborate to complete an inference task. Each split model except for the last one produces intermediate results of inference, and the result is serialized and transmitted to the next edge in the pipeline. Hence, any 'central' edge's roles as both the gRPC client that requests the next inference to the neighbor and the gRPC server help complete the remaining inference task in response to the other client's request. In the future, we aim to adopt more lightweight methods for serialization in terms of conversion cost and transmission size overhead. However, for this study, the built-in serialization method of Tensorflow was used. The inference agent splits the model when the model slicer requests it with the split point. In the current implementation, the agent splits the model using the Tensorflow method.

Figure 3 shows the detailed architecture of the inference agent. We considered three elements to develop a realistic inference. The first is the latency. We set an artificial latency by using Linux traffic control, 'tc.' The command was set to each docker container with modified latency. This latency applies to both inbound and outbound of each inference agent. Therefore, based on our environment, which is composed of three inferences—device, edge, and cloud—the cloud has high latency, while the others have low latency.

We also considered the overhead to show the hardware's limitations. The realistic simulation needs to show better performance in the cloud and poor performance in the device. The overhead is implemented through the Python

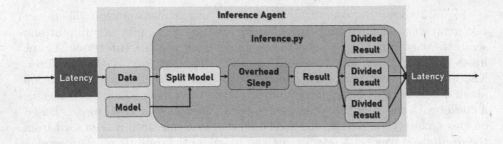

Fig. 3. Architecture of the inference agent

sleep method. When the agent process the data, it measures the processing time. With the given overhead ratio, it calculates the overhead time based on the formula, $(OverheadTime) = (OverheadRatio) * (ProcessTime)$.

The last consideration was throughput, which roughly simulates the maximum network bandwidth and congestion status. We limit the maximum throughput and divide the tensor if the size exceeds the throughput. In that case, of course, the next inference agent collects it and reassembles it.

4 Experiment Setting

4.1 Research Questions

In this section, we outline our research questions to find valuable insights that explain the consequences of different split points and network configurations

- **RQ 1:** How do the different choices of split points in the CNN model layers influence the inference quality?
- **RQ 2:** How does change in network configurations affect different split point settings?
- **RQ 3:** What would be the best decision strategy for choosing better split points while considering application goals?

4.2 Experiments Setup

We used a sequential CNN model consisting of 14 layers for this experiment. Table 1 shows the layer construction of the model in tf.Keras type. This model is constructed with five convolutional layers (Conv2D) and three pooling layers (MaxPooling2D). We set up the two split points for the experiment, one for between the device and edge and the other for between edge and cloud.

We set several candidates for each split point (both device-side and cloudside) based on our prior knowledge of CNN layers. The split point between the device and edge has two candidates: after the first Conv2D layer (layer 1) and after the first MaxPooling2D layer (layer 3). The choice of either split point involves a

Table 1. The elementary CNN model for experiment

#	Layer	Output shape	Param #
1	Conv2D	(None, 26, 26, 32)	320
2	Conv2D	(None, 24, 24, 64)	18,496
3	MaxPooling2D	(None, 12, 12, 64)	0
4	BatchNormalization	(None, 12, 12, 128)	256
5	Conv2D	(None, 10, 10, 128)	73,856
6	Conv2D	(None, 8, 8, 128)	147,584
7	MaxPooling2D	(None, 4, 4, 128)	0
8	BatchNormalization	(None, 4, 4, 128)	512
9	Conv2D	(None, 2, 2, 256)	295,168
10	MaxPooling2D	(None, 1, 1, 256)	0
11	Flatten	(None, 256)	0
12	BatchNormalization	(None, 256)	1,024
13	Dense	(None, 512)	131,584
14	Dense	(None, 10)	5,130

trade-off: a split point after layer 1 can achieve better performance because the device has much more overhead (x10) than edge and cloud. However, choosing to split after layer 3 affects the network bandwidth because the size of tensors passed through the pooling layer would become much smaller. The split point between the edge and the cloud has four candidates: after the second Batch-Normalization layer (layer 8), after the 5th Conv2D layer (layer 9), after the 3rd MaxPooling2D layer (layer 10), or after the Flatten layer (layer 11). A split point after layer 8 or layer 9 would utilize better computation power on the cloud but tends to have greater network latency because of the high tensor dimension. On the other hand, a split point after layer 10 or 11 would reduce the transmitted tensor size while having to compute more on medium-end edges.

Table 2. Experiment configuration

Config	Variable	Device	Edge	Cloud
All	Overhead	x10	x5	x1
	Frames	50		
Type 1	Latency (ms)	2.5	2.5	250
	Max throughput	500,000	500,000	500,000
Type 2	Latency (ms)	2.5	2.5	250
	Max throughput	**50,000**	**50,000**	**50,000**
Type 3	Latency (ms)	2.5	2.5	**1000**
	Max throughput	500,000	500,000	500,000

22   E. Cho et al.

Table 2 shows the configuration of the experiment. The unit of the max throughput set is the length of the serialized string of tensors. The overhead is $x10$, $x5$, and $x1$ for each inference to reflect each device's performance limitations, edge, and cloud. Each test is conducted with 50 data frames. We set three configuration types. The first configuration is a primary setting with a latency of 2.5 ms and 250 ms with a maximum throughput of 500,000. The second configuration has an environment with low maximum throughput, causing the packet size to be smaller and the transmission frequency to be higher. The last configuration has high latency (1000 ms) in the case of the wide area network (WAN) suffering from low quality or congestion. We referred to the general range of the latency of WAN as being from 250 ms to 500 ms.

5   Result

Here, we report the measured processing time of 50 frames and frame drop rate with three configurations explained in the previous section (Figs. 4, 5 and Tables 3, 4, 5).

Table 3. Experiment result with configuration 1

Split point	Time (s)	Frame drop
Conv2D - BatchNormalization	49.7454	0.18
Conv2D - Conv2D	49.7391	0.14
Conv2D - MaxPooling2D	49.7301	0.34
Conv2D - Flatten	49.8100	0.18
MaxPooling2D - BatchNormalization	49.8244	0.16
MaxPooling2D - Conv2D	49.8072	0.18
MaxPooling2D - MaxPooling2D	50.2666	0.22
MaxPooling2D - Flatten	49.5615	0.20

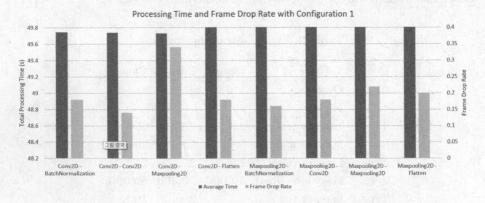

Fig. 4. Graph of processing time and frame drop rate with configuration 1

Table 4. Experiment result with configuration 2

Split point	Time (s)	Frame drop
Conv2D - BatchNormalization	50.7831	0.68
Conv2D - Conv2D	49.5615	0.78
Conv2D - MaxPooling2D	50.2550	0.62
Conv2D - Flatten	50.2487	0.64
MaxPooling2D - BatchNormalization	49.3895	0.68
MaxPooling2D - Conv2D	49.3894	0.66
MaxPooling2D - MaxPooling2D	48.3246	0.56
MaxPooling2D - Flatten	47.8205	0.60

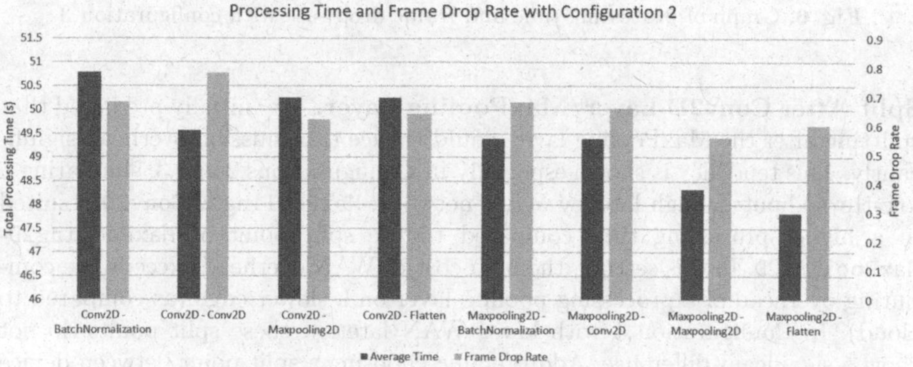

Fig. 5. Graph of processing time and frame drop rate with configuration 2

Table 5. Experiment result with configuration 3

Split point	Time (s)	Frame drop
Conv2D - BatchNormalization	49.8217	0.28
Conv2D - Conv2D	49.7521	0.22
Conv2D - MaxPooling2D	49.7888	0.08
Conv2D - Flatten	49.7549	0.08
MaxPooling2D - BatchNormalization	49.8062	0.14
MaxPooling2D - Conv2D	49.7817	0.08
MaxPooling2D - MaxPooling2D	49.7446	0.12
MaxPooling2D - Flatten	49.7721	0.10

5.1 RQ1: Better Split Points Regarding the Type of CNN Layer

Here, to answer the first research question, we verify our initial assumption on the trade-off between network cost and computational overhead on each edge/device from our experiment result.

24   E. Cho et al.

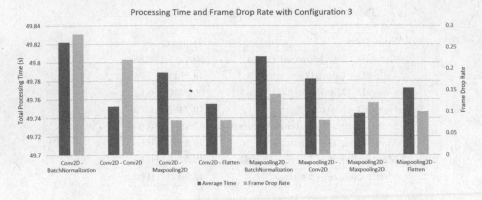

Fig. 6. Graph of processing time and frame drop rate with configuration 3

Split After Conv2D Layer/MaxPooling Layer. We initially predicted that splitting after the MaxPooling layer would reduce transmission overhead significantly. This tendency is shown especially in Configurations 2 and 3, simulating a low-throughput or high-latency WAN network. `MaxPooling2D-Conv2D` resulted in a higher processing time compared to the split point of `MaxPooling2D-MaxPooling2D`. In this setting, the high cost of WAN overhead exceeds the computing overhead of a processing pooling layer on a slower edge (as compared to cloud). In Configuration 1 with lower WAN latency, these split points do not show a significant difference. Additionally, choosing a split point between device and edge did not reveal much difference because we set LAN latency as only 2.5 ms (although this value is in the range of general LAN latency) (Fig. 6).

Overall, the result was more affected by the network configuration than by the characteristics of layers. However, with a greater penalty on large tensor transmission, the benefit of transmitting more processed tensors by doing more computation on device/edge would be discovered.

5.2   RQ2: Effect of Network Configurations

As shown in the previous subsection, different network configurations would result in divergent processing time and frame drop rate. With Configuration 2, lowering the max throughput caused high frame drop rate because packets flooded the network. Again, reducing the transmission size by processing more layers on the device/edge would prevent the total processing time from going up too high, but it could not reduce the frame drop rate.

5.3   RQ3: Application Goal-Driven DNN Slicing

The processing overhead (fixed in this experiment) could be tuned because nowadays, both cloud and edge devices can scale using a useful hypervisor technique (e.g., Docker). Hence, based on the simulation results and target applications' requirements, we can manipulate allocated computing power on each machine rather than sacrifice its goal. Preserving the application goal is essential because, for safety-critical applications like visual inference in an autonomous car, frame drops in a relatively short period can result in severe situations (e.g., not identifying pedestrians in front of a car).

5.4 Limitation and Future Work

Initially, we planned to investigate a more diverse setting with varied computing overhead settings, different throughput for LAN and WAN, and more diverse distribution of latency. Unfortunately, we found that there are too many parameters to effectively tune. Hence, we decided to focus on a specific and representative set of latency and throughput settings and tried to explain the consequences of different split points from the perspective of the target application's requirements and the characteristics of the CNN model. Our settings based on fixed values can constrain the expressiveness of the realistic environment in our simulator. However, we concluded that we could still produce a subset of valuable characteristics in combining various split points and network configurations, including high latency and low throughput on WAN. We set a slightly extreme value to observe the difference more clearly. (In a low-throughput setting, every batched frame was split up into 20 packets, and the value of 1000 ms is quite a harsh value simulating a very congested or erroneous network.)

In future work, we plan to implement a more fine-grained model slicer for the general Tensorflow model that contains more complex components, such as residual blocks to cope with a more realistic model and dataset. Supporting non-sequential models required non-trivial engineering, which is hard to accomplish. However, doing so would make our simulation environment more practical for pre-validating split points and preliminarily deciding which models to use and how much computation power is needed to achieve the required performance. We also aim to automate the steps to find the best configuration of parameters using search methods such as genetic algorithms (GAs). This approach can be uniquely conducted on our framework because we support a full software configuration in a single Docker daemon environment.

6 Conclusion

We propose a fully software-configurable simulation framework for DNN slicing on edges. The simulation environment works on general sequential-type DNN models, and arbitrary latency and throughput can be injected into the framework. Computational overhead on each machine can be simulated as well. Through an experiment with three different network configurations, we gained insight on how to consider CNN layer characteristics when deciding on split points. The experiment also showed that the total processing time and frame drop rate significantly depend on network capacity. We put a value in our simulator to provide an effective means of cost estimation in constructing a DNN inference pipeline utilizing edges—this achieves the idea of *adapting machines* for the application's requirements.

Acknowledgement. This research was supported by the MSIT (Ministry of Science and ICT), Korea, under the ITRC (Information Technology Research Center) support program (IITP-2021-2020-0-01795) and (No. 2015-0-00250, (SW Star Lab) Software R&D for Model-based Analysis and Verification of Higher-order Large Complex System) supervised by the IITP (Institute of Information & Communications Technology Planning & Evaluation).

References

1. Fowers, J., et al.: A configurable cloud-scale DNN processor for real-time AI. In: 2018 ACM/IEEE 45th Annual International Symposium on Computer Architecture (ISCA), pp. 1–14. IEEE (2018)
2. Hsu, K.J., Bhardwaj, K., Gavrilovska, A.: Couper: DNN model slicing for visual analytics containers at the edge. In: Proceedings of the 4th ACM/IEEE Symposium on Edge Computing, pp. 179–194 (2019)
3. Lockhart, L., Harvey, P., Imai, P., Willis, P., Varghese, B.: Scission: performance-driven and context-aware cloud-edge distribution of deep neural networks. In: 2020 IEEE/ACM 13th International Conference on Utility and Cloud Computing (UCC), pp. 257–268. IEEE (2020)
4. Ren, P., Qiao, X., Huang, Y., Liu, L., Dustdar, S., Chen, J.: Edge-assisted distributed DNN collaborative computing approach for mobile web augmented reality in 5G networks. IEEE Network **34**(2), 254–261 (2020)
5. Teerapittayanon, S., McDanel, B., Kung, H.T.: Distributed deep neural networks over the cloud, the edge and end devices. In: IEEE 37th International Conference on Distributed Computing Systems (ICDCS), pp. 328–339 (2017)
6. Talagala, N., et al.: ECO: harmonizing edge and cloud with ML/DL orchestration. In: USENIX Workshop on Hot Topics in Edge Computing (HotEdge 2018) (2018)
7. Tao, Z., Li, Q.: ESGD: communication efficient distributed deep learning on the edge. In: USENIX Workshop on Hot Topics in Edge Computing (HotEdge 2018) (2018)
8. Teerapittayanon, S., McDanel, B., Kung, H.T.: Distributed deep neural networks over the cloud, the edge and end devices. In: 2017 IEEE 37th International Conference on Distributed Computing Systems (ICDCS), pp. 328–339. IEEE (2017)
9. Wang, X., Luo, Y., Crankshaw, D., Tumanov, A., Yu, F., Gonzalez, J.E.: IDK cascades: fast deep learning by learning not to overthink. arXiv preprint arXiv:1706.00885 (2017)

Towards Proactive Context-Aware IoT Environments by Means of Federated Learning

Rubén Rentero-Trejo[✉][iD], Daniel Flores-Martin[iD], Jaime Galán-Jiménez[iD], José García-Alonso[iD], Juan Manuel Murillo[iD], and Javier Berrocal[iD]

University of Extremadura, Cáceres, Spain
{rrenterot,dfloresm,jaime,jgaralo,juanmamu,jberolm}@unex.es

Abstract. Internet of Things (IoT) integrates billions of smart devices and keeps growing. IoT technologies play a crucial role in smart applications that improve the quality of life. Likewise, the computational capacity of mobile devices has greatly increased, opening up new possibilities. In many cases, human interaction is necessary for IoT devices to perform properly. Users must configure more and more devices, investing time and effort. Artificial Intelligence (AI) techniques are currently used to predict user needs and behavior, trying to adapt devices to user preferences. However, achieving all-purpose models is a challenging task, aggravated by long training periods preventing personalized models in the early stages. This paper proposes a solution based on Federated Learning to predict behaviors in different environments and improve user's coexistence with IoT devices, avoiding most manual interactions and making use of mobile devices capabilities. Federation allows new users' predictions to be done using other users' previous behaviors in similar environments. Also, it provides closer customization, immediate availability and avoids most manual device interactions.

Keywords: Federated learning · Mobile devices · Context-aware · IoT

1 Introduction

There are currently 12 billion connected IoT devices [13] and nearly 4 billion smartphones around the world [19]. These devices come equipped with complex sensors, computing, and communication capabilities. The amount of information handled by end devices opens up endless possibilities when it comes to how IoT can improve our lives. Some of the areas in continuous development are healthcare, industry, energy solutions, or mobility [22].

More and more users are using IoT devices in their daily lives, and concepts such as Smart-Home [1] or Smart-cities [2] are emerging. These specialized devices often need configuration and human interaction to achieve their most optimal performance. However, with the growing number of devices [13], it is becoming more difficult to manage them properly without investing a lot of time.

© Springer Nature Switzerland AG 2022
M. Bakaev et al. (Eds.): ICWE 2021 Workshops, CCIS 1508, pp. 27–38, 2022.
https://doi.org/10.1007/978-3-030-92231-3_3

In addition, when a user adds new devices, the effort increases accordingly. This may reduce the perceived benefits of IoT.

Edge and Mist Computing (EC, MC) techniques bring computing and decision making closer to the data source. They have driven solutions to low latency requirements, context awareness or distributed computing to provide a good quality of service [8], especially with the rise of AI and Deep Learning (DL). Federated Learning (FL) emerges with this spirit and improves DL to go a step further in achieving these goals.

Several works study the statistical heterogeneity of user data in FL [11,12,27] but do not attempt to find a personalized solution for each user. Others are based on large recommender systems leading to heavy architectures [4,10], making them hard to deploy in cost-effective devices with lower specifications, usually present in this kind of environments. Some solutions define behavior based on rule sets [10], but they are limited, do not cover all possible cases, and do not adapt dynamically to new situations. Approaches are needed to deal with any user and environment without heavy deployments and long adaptation periods.

This paper proposes a solution based on FL where mobile devices have two models. First, a global model has the knowledge generated in the federation and enables predictions to new users and new environments. Second, a personalized model which adjusts to the needs of the particular user for already known environments. Both models can be retrained to meet the needs of the federation and the users. This approach allows fast personalization and deployments, being able to offer predictions in every environment the user visits.

The rest of the document is structured as follows. Section 2 presents our motivations. Section 3 explains our proposal, divided into Data Model and Architecture. Section 4 presents the experimental scenario, setup and results. Section 5 presents related works. Finally, concluding remarks are given in Sect. 6.

2   Motivation

IoT devices make people's lives easier by specializing and automating a wide variety of tasks. Nowadays, it is easy to find devices such as light bulbs, locks, TVs, wearables, among many other examples in any workplace or home environment.

Managing each device is a simple task after the initial configuration. However, when the number increases, the device management becomes more difficult and time-consuming. If we analyze most IoT devices, their functionality is based on running specific, direct and not very complex commands. Usually linked to a user's habits or patterns repeated over time and with minimal variations. Thus if we know the actions to be performed, we can automate them, avoiding the user from being concerned about constant interactions. In short, we need a system to make decisions in place of users.

The behavior is device and environment-dependent and can be reproduced for similar devices in similar environments. We call *environment* the set of different IoT devices and the circumstances around them (e.g. time, place, mode, patterns, etc.). Common examples are workplaces or home environments, usually with very different conditions. Therefore, it is concluded that a person will move through different environments, and automation should persist in all of them, always adapted to the user's preferences and the environment.

To better understand this problem, an example is proposed below: *Suppose a user named John, a technology enthusiast who commonly interacts with IoT devices. John wakes up every morning at the same time, turns on the lights and gets ready for work. After finishing, he turns off all devices and goes to his office. During working hours, he prefers a specific light and temperature, as well as background music to help him concentrate. When he arrives home, he wants his devices to recognize his arrival, turn on the lights, and tune the TV to his favorite channel. John has tried programming his devices to trigger at specific times but his schedule is flexible and do not achieve the desired behavior. He usually sleeps late, but recently has more work than usual and decides to go to sleep earlier, so he must turn off the TV and lights manually. Changes in his schedule required him to set up multiple configurations and manual changes, which makes John wonder if the deployment of smart devices is worth it.*

As shown, approaches that learn from user behavior and contextual information are needed to automate actions without requiring users to reconfigure devices every time their needs change. The availability should be immediate from the model's acquisition, so it would not be reasonable to offer a model which requires long adaptation periods. Recommendation systems offer a partial solution to these situations; however, dependence on cloud services causes high latency, issues in low connectivity situations and privacy concerns. In this context, MC solutions that can make decisions locally without sharing sensitive data are desirable. Furthermore, high hardware requirements lead to higher economical costs for users who wish to deploy a central element in their environment, limited to a geographical area and unavailable in other places, reinforcing the Mist alternative.

While avoiding cloud alternatives, it is necessary to solve how to allow knowledge to travel between different environments, since the system needs to operate in all of them. Since the beginning of this century, smartphones have been classified as personal objects that accompanies people in their daily activities [25]. They are the users' closest elements and where we must focus the learning process. In addition, considering the computational possibilities, capacity and data traffic currently handled by these devices, they present a promising option to address this problem by meeting the requirements for Machine Learning (ML). Therefore, mobile devices will be the main learning nodes and will act as storage and as information vehicles, capable of moving between environments. This solution would allow John to change environments freely, transfer previously acquired knowledge to a new environment and use it to make new decisions.

To ensure new users fast deployments and customization tasks, we will make use of the *global knowledge* offered by FL. FL is a learning technique that allows mobile devices to collaboratively learn a shared prediction model by keeping all training data on the device, sharing only gradients or weights, instead of raw data. It enables smarter models, low latency, lower power consumption, ability to use the model immediately and personalization based on device usage, all while improving privacy [15].

Dealing with a mobile environment means dealing with Non-IID [28], unbalanced and massively distributed data, problems that do not occur in centralized environments. We are in a situation where each user has different preferences, actions, favourited devices, etc. This nature has a high impact on traditional ML models [9,18] and is one of the reasons to use FL and the Federated Averaging (FedAvg) algorithm, a generalization of FedSGD [23]. FedAvg exchanges the updated weights without sharing personal data, and performs an average among the participants to obtain a generalized model [15], showing good results in these situations [16].

Usually in FL, once the global model is complete, it is provided to users by transferring weights and retrained to perform the personalization. First, this presents difficulties assimilating subsequent changes in the federation since if this transfer is performed, the personalization already obtained would be lost and the local model would return to the starting point of the global model. Second, the model must address very different situations: regular users and environments on the one hand, and new users and environments on the other.

Therefore, we present a solution with a double model. The global model has the federation's knowledge and will evolve with it. The strength of this model is its ability to offer predictions to new users and those who encounter new environments. The local model has the knowledge of the individual user. It aims to obtain the highest possible degree of personalization to provide effective predictions. This way, any kind of user can deal with any kind of environment.

By keeping two independent models, the user is always allowed to have a copy of the global model existing on the server, which is constantly being updated and is sensitive to changes in the federation (e.g. trends, new uses, patterns). All this without affecting personalization on the local model.

Thanks to this approach, devices will receive commands and automatically react based on each user preferences, making them focus only on new or exceptional situations that do not follow a usual behavior pattern, greatly reducing the user's manual actions and facilitating his coexistence with the IoT devices around the user.

3   Proactive Context-Aware IoT Environments

As discussed in the previous section, there is a need to exploit mobile devices potential and integrate them into the IoT ecosystem using techniques such as FL, avoiding high dependency on the cloud. Two models are needed to address very different situations: a global model collaboratively trained which generalizes the federation behavior, while another model of similar features is in charge of carrying out the personalization of user behaviors. The first model allows new users to have a starting point for decision making while the second model has personalization as its objective, achieving decision making adapted to the preferences of the particular user.

This section is divided into two: first, *data model* analysis to deal with IoT environments, user preferences and the difficulties they present, and second, the required *architecture* with a dual learning model.

3.1   Data Model

The following are the most important functions to be performed by the model and the data groups required to develop them (Table 1).

- Needs to identify IoT devices within the same environment and then generalize that behavior to new scenarios where the **environment**, or even the user himself, is different.
- **Device type** is specified to distinguish behaviors between different devices (e.g. actions performed on a TV from those performed on a light bulb).
- **Device ID** to complement the above since there may be several devices of the same type in one environment and it is essential to differentiate them.
- **Connection type** to send actions. It does not affect decision making but it is needed to allow effective action forwarding to the devices in the future.
- The **action** specifies the direct command to be executed on the IoT device and is the target variable for predictions.
- The **probability** or reliability level is associated with the final predictions. It will be used later to finally decide on the action to be taken.
- The model must be able to understand the temporal aspect of events and identify patterns based on them. For now, the identified behaviors are those related to **hours** of the day (e.g. 8:00, 15:00) and **weekdays** (workdays, weekends, free days), but can be extended to long term patterns such as seasons of the year.
- Finally, a method is needed to indicate the user presence (**arrival**) and can be implemented through mobile device location, being transparent to him. This information is useful to control time patterns, where a prediction must be performed but the user is not in the environment. It must be evaluated if the execution of the action makes sense when the user is not present.

From a data perspective, we call *usual environments* (UE) to those statistically predominant in the user's dataset. Similarly, *new environments* (NE) are those with insufficient or no data. After a previous analysis of possible user behaviors, we identified 3 different situations: 1) The user is in his UE and requests predictions for an already known environment; 2) The user requests predictions after changing to a NE (not usual or unknown) where devices or interactions are different; 3) A new user with no previous information. This last case, for practical purposes, can be interpreted as a NE.

3.2   Architecture

The main learning approach consists of neural networks (NNs), which serve as the basis for the two models that will be explained throughout this section:

Table 1. Example tuples extracted during data collection.

Env.	Device ID	Device type	Connection type	Action	Time	Arrival	Prob.
Home	AC1	Air-conditioner	WiFi	24 °C	2019-10-14 at 15:07:51 CEST	False	95%
Home	TV1	SMARTTV	WiFi	Tele5	2019-10-14 at 22:00:03 CEST	True	80%
Office	S2	SPEAKER	BLE	Turn on	2019-10-20 at 09:05:10 CEST	True	75%

1) a local model to achieve personalization; 2) a global model to achieve adaptability to new situations. NNs have been selected given FL's ease for working with them and address inherent problems with ML in this type of situations [18].

Our solution is based on standard FL and *FedAvg*, adapted to use a dual model. On the one hand, a model is in charge of performing all the usual FL tasks (GM in Fig. 1). Its goal is to create a global model from the knowledge of the federation users, then downloaded to the user's device and used as a global knowledge base. On the other hand, a local model with similar characteristics to the previous one (LM in Fig. 1), created on the device itself, is in charge of training only with user data and without interference from external models (as in FL) to achieve a personalized behavior.

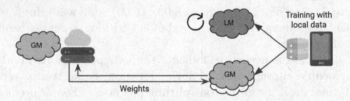

Fig. 1. FL with a double local model architecture. Global model (GM) runs FL as usual, local model (LM) does the personalization.

The *global model* is the one built from the knowledge of the entire network of users. Initially, each user has an empty model that is initialized by a set of parameters defined in the server (e.g. epochs, learning rate, etc.), providing greater control of the server over the federation. Then, it is trained for several epochs, and the NN weights are serialized into an update package and sent to the server. This process occurs with all connected devices, and the server aggregates all packages to create the global model. This process is repeated until the set rounds or until the desired accuracy is obtained. At the end of the process, the user obtains this global model to provide a starting point for predictions.

This method allows devices to make predictions based on the general federation behavior. It is especially useful in situations where new users join the federation. Since there is no previous information about them, they do not have a personalized model to request predictions from. However, this global model allows predictions to be made, in exchange for a small penalty in the accuracy of the predictions. As for the aggregations carried out in the server, with FedAvg, each of the NN weights will be determined by the result of averaging the weights of NNs located in each device (McMahan et al. [15]).

During tests, some models were unable to learn in one round. Hence, leading to a negative impact on the global model from low-quality weights. To solve this problem, those models are not aggregated and are given additional rounds to improve. After including this pre-selection and observing the improvements in accuracy, we conclude that a model unable to learn and provide solutions for its user, would not do it for the rest. This is used to prevent global model poisoning and as a preventive measure against malicious participants.

The *local model* is the one located and isolated in the device, i.e. this model will not be affected by the actions performed in the federation. It trains with device local data, in the same way that the downloaded global model does. However, this model does not share its weights with any server and remains independent of the federated environment. This model objective is to obtain the highest degree of personalization (skew) possible from device usage. This model benefit lies in situations where the user is in one of his UEs to make accurate predictions adjusted to his preferences.

In short, the global model serves as a source of general knowledge, basically, the actions that would be taken by the federation in a similar situation. Eventually, the global model will be replaced by the personalized model, which best knows the particular user behavior. Both models compete to offer the best predictions; if one cannot give a sufficiently accurate prediction, the model's prediction with the highest reliability index for that situation will be chosen.

4   Validation

4.1   Scenario

A case study has been proposed with situations similar to the example given in Sect. 2. A set of real users who regularly interact with IoT devices have been selected. Notable differences between them are work and leisure schedules (hours and weekdays), device type preferences, usage, environment changes and occasional patterns. They have been provided with an Android app to specify the device, performed action, and environment. Remainder data from Sect. 3.1 is automatically taken. This app only serves as an information-gathering tool and does not perform any real action with IoT devices.

The system has been implemented using TensorFlow (TF)[1]. However, since TFLite from TF only performs inference on Android devices, this part has been implemented with the DeepLearning4j library[2]. Apart from system performance, the aim is to study device computational and battery consumption.

---

[1] https://www.tensorflow.org/.
[2] https://deeplearning4j.org/.

4.2   Set-Up

During data gathering, users had all possible options within the following limits: 4 environments, 5 different device types, 12 devices, 2 connection modes, and 10 actions in total. This phase lasted 3 weeks. Figure 2 shows the different distributions of actions and the variability in the total amount of data. There is a total of 6 users and 1,313 tuples obtained.

After an exhaustive data processing, each dataset has a total of 64 columns, generated from the source data by *One-Hot Encoding*, 54 of them will be taken as input features for NNs. Since we are dealing with a classification problem, the output data are 10 classes. As for the NN configuration, the input layer has 54 nodes, followed by two hidden layers with the same number of nodes and ending with an output layer with a total of 10 nodes, corresponding to the actions to be predicted. All layers have *ReLu* activation function, except for the output layer that has a *Softmax* one. Some additional configurations are the SGD optimizer, *learning rate* of 0.015, *momentum* of 0.9 and *decay* = $\frac{lr}{n\_rounds}$. Iterations are 5 *epochs* and $n\_rounds = 100$. During the testing period, a wide range of hyperparameters, network configurations, network depths and techniques such as *dropout* or *batch normalization* were tested, however, the configuration with the best final results is the one described above.

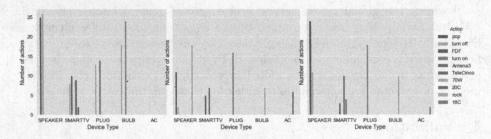

Fig. 2. Data distributions, preferences and total data across 3 different clients.

For the testing phase and since we need enough data to train, we kept 50% of the data obtained from each user, randomly taken and used to request predictions from the two models. The monitoring of mobile devices has been carried out with Android Profiler [5] and Battery Historian [6].

4.3   Results

The progress of both the global model and the personalized local models has been monitored. In Fig. 3b we can see the differences between local ones: Some models (clients 1, 3, 4, 5) learn quickly the behavior of their users, reaching accuracy rates higher than 90%. However, there are some models (clients 0, 2) that do not learn properly. The main cause are users with no apparent behavioral patterns or who interact with IoT devices in an occasional and random way that would be impossible to predict, cases already considered in the data collection phase and classified as outliers. After seeing the performance of local models and their accuracies, we consider the customization rate to be successful and satisfactorily adapted to the user's needs.

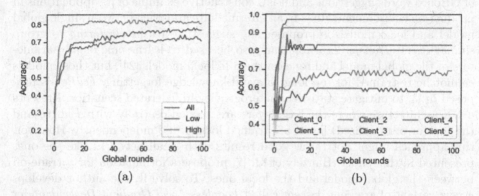

Fig. 3. Accuracy. (a) Global model accuracy: all clients aggregated, low and high requirements filter (65% and 75% min. accuracy). (b) Model accuracy of 6 different users and their local models.

As for the global model, the initial tests were performed with all available users (Fig. 3a), allowing the server to aggregate any model regardless of its quality. With this, an accuracy of 74% has been achieved in the global model facing situations in new environments. Being aware that there are local models incapable of learning from their users (i.e. outliers) causing poisoning of the global model, a quality filter was implemented before aggregation. After testing with pre-selection, the global model increases its accuracy to 83%, improving its convergence and requiring fewer training rounds.

The small percentage of cases where models do not give an accurate prediction is caused by situations where it is difficult to provide one. For example, loudspeakers, if a user listens to pop and rock music with the same frequency.

Apart from the system's performance, we are particularly interested in the impact this learning process has on mobile devices. Data obtained are listed below. The Android Profiler report shows a CPU usage of 19% and a RAM usage of 130 MB on average. As for network usage, each update package is 25 KB in size, sent in 10 rounds (250 KB data sent and 250 KB data received), for a total of 0.52 MB of network traffic taking network headers into account, and bandwidth highest peak of 110 KB/s. The execution time has an average duration of 11 s. Regarding the battery impact, we obtained results of 0.04% usage of device's battery, classified by Battery Historian as a low-level cost. As for the inference cost (i.e. a prediction), we consider it insignificant as it is so small that it is not even recorded in the history.

5   Related Work

There is plenty of statistical heterogeneity works [11,12,27] who study the impact of No-IID data and propose new algorithms like *SCAFFOLD*, but they do not try to achieve a personalized behavior. In [26], FL is used to improve the quality of GBoard word suggestions and it is a constructive example of its applications in production environments. In [14], an intermediate approach between single global model and local models is proposed, by suggesting a *user clustering* to group similar users. *Transfer Learning* can also be used to learn some or all parameters in the global model and re-learn them in local models [24], but those models cannot be re-trained for too long to avoid knowledge forgetting. *FedPer* is proposed in [3] to mitigate statistical heterogeneity in federated scenarios. Presents a NN architecture where the base layers are trained centrally with *FedAvg* and the top (or personalized) layers are trained locally and independently. However, this approach might not throw good results with small networks like the ones presented in this paper. Hanzely et al. [7] propose a formulation for a trade-off between the global model and the local ones. To solve it, the author develops a new variant of gradient descent called *Loopless Local Gradient Descent* under the claim that standard *FedAvg* might be too aggressive.

Cook and Das [4] propose a complete architecture for smart environments which goes beyond the learning node discussed in this paper and achieved good results, while Kabir et al. [10] purposes another architecture for different areas at home, but neither of them discusses situations outside those environments and how to deal with different ones. While Think Home [20] is deployable on cheap hardware like Arduino boards, it is more focused on the administration and power-saving topic, and does not try to automate behaviors with future predictions. Nascimiento et al. [17] propose a system with both general and specific models and switch between them, but it is based only on one feature. Finally, [21] propose a system which personalizes users behavior inside their environment achieving good results. However, it highly depends on the server to train their models and needs a training phase before users can use their models.

6   Discussion and Conclusions

The increasing number of IoT devices and smart environments will make this paradigm difficult for users to manage due to the high number of interactions and configuration that they require. This will result in users spending too much time on devices' management and the final benefits of this paradigm being reduced. To reduce this effort, users need support tools automating or semi-automating their to reduce the workload and the interaction level with their devices, keeping the workload to the minimum. In this paper, a dual model to predict interactions with IoT devices in different environments, based on users preferences, has been proposed. This proposal makes use of contextual information and previous actions of federated users and has a low impact on mobile devices.

During the development of this work, the following key aspects have been identified: 1) Intelligent environments can be very different and heterogeneous, which makes developing a multipurpose and effective model for any context a challenging task. Besides, interoperability is crucial to allow easy management of any IoT device using a mobile device; 2) Context and properties of environments shape their fingerprint. Each environment is defined by the devices in them and how they are used, assisting the model in its task of environment identification; 3) The more contextual properties and information to be analyzed, the more appropriate the behavior will be, and more similar environments can be identified. A better understanding of context leads to smarter models and better predictions. However, if all possible features were taken into account, we would incur a problem that goes beyond the high cardinality in classification problems, i.e. an infinite or undefined cardinality. Since there will always be new devices, features and actions, it is hard to provide a standard input for NNs to obtain outcomes for every potential environment in the federation. Therefore, this first proof of concept is limited to several features. Techniques such as *zero-shot learning* could shed light on this problem, but further research is needed.

In future works, we plan to apply the proposed approach in social environments, where different users need to be taken into account and conflicts of interests need to be addressed.

Acknowledgement. This work was funded by the project RTI2018-094591-B-I00 and the FPU17/02251 grant (MCI /AEI/FEDER, UE), the 4IE+ Project (0499-4IE-PLUS-4-E) funded by the Interreg V-A España-Portugal (POCTEP) 2014–2020 program, by the Department of Economy, Science and Digital Agenda of the Government of Extremadura (GR18112, IB18030), and by the European Regional Development Fund.

References

1. Alaa, M., Zaidan, A.A., Zaidan, B.B., Talal, M., Kiah, M.L.: A review of smart home applications based on Internet of Things. J. Netw. Comput. Appl. **97**, 48–65 (2017). https://doi.org/10.1016/j.jnca.2017.08.017
2. Arasteh, H., et al.: IoT-based smart cities: a survey. In: IEEE-EEEIC 2016, pp. 1–6 (2016). https://doi.org/10.1109/EEEIC.2016.7555867
3. Arivazhagan, M.G., Aggarwal, V., Singh, A.K., Choudhary, S.: Federated learning with personalization layers (2019)
4. Cook, D.J., Youngblood, M., Das, S.K.: A multi-agent approach to controlling a smart environment. In: Augusto, J.C., Nugent, C.D. (eds.) Designing Smart Homes. LNCS (LNAI), vol. 4008, pp. 165–182. Springer, Heidelberg (2006). https://doi.org/10.1007/11788485_10
5. Google Inc.: Measure app performance with Android Profiler, October 2020. https://developer.android.com/studio/profile/android-profiler
6. Google Inc.: Profile battery usage with Batterystats and Battery Historian, January 2021. https://developer.android.com/topic/performance/power/setup-battery-historian
7. Hanzely, F., Richtárik, P.: Federated learning of a mixture of global and local models (2021)
8. Herrera, J.L., Bellavista, P., Foschini, L., Galán-Jiménez, J., Murillo, J.M., Berrocal, J.: Meeting stringent QoS requirements in IIoT based scenarios. In: GLOBECOM 2020–2020 IEEE Global Communications Conference, pp. 1–6. IEEE (2020)

9. Hsieh, K., Phanishayee, A., Mutlu, O., Gibbons, P.B.: The non-IID data quagmire of decentralized machine learning. In: ICML (2020)
10. Kabir, M.H., Hoque, M.R., Yang, S.H.: Development of a smart home context-aware application: a machine learning based approach. Int. J. Smart Home **9**, 217–226 (2015). https://doi.org/10.14257/ijsh.2015.9.1.23
11. Karimireddy, S.P., Kale, S., Mohri, M., Reddi, S.J., Stich, S.U., Suresh, A.T.: SCAFFOLD: stochastic controlled averaging for federated learning (2020)
12. Li, X., Huang, K., Yang, W., Wang, S., Zhang, Z.: On the convergence of FedAvg on non-IID data. In: ICLR (2020). https://openreview.net/forum?id=HJxNAnVtDS
13. Lueth, K.L.: State of the IoT 2020: 12 billion IoT connections, November 2020. https://iot-analytics.com/state-of-the-iot-2020-12-billion-iot-connections-surpassing-non-iot-for-the-first-time/
14. Mansour, Y., Mohri, M., Ro, J., Suresh, A.T.: Three approaches for personalization with applications to federated learning (2020)
15. McMahan, H., Moore, E., Ramage, D., Agüera y Arcas, B.: Federated learning of deep networks using model averaging. ArXiv abs/1602.05629 (2016)
16. McMahan, H., Moore, E., Ramage, D., Hampson, S., Agüera y Arcas, B.: Communication-efficient learning of deep networks from decentralized data. In: AISTATS (2017)
17. Nascimento, N., Alencar, P., Lucena, C., Cowan, D.: A context-aware machine learning-based approach, October 2018
18. Nigam, N., Dutta, T., Gupta, H.P.: Impact of noisy labels in learning techniques: a survey. In: Kolhe, M.L., Tiwari, S., Trivedi, M.C., Mishra, K.K. (eds.) Advances in Data and Information Sciences. LNNS, vol. 94, pp. 403–411. Springer, Singapore (2020). https://doi.org/10.1007/978-981-15-0694-9_38
19. O'Dea, S.: Smartphone users 2020, December 2020. https://www.statista.com/statistics/330695/number-of-smartphone-users-worldwide/
20. Reinisch, C., Kofler, M.J., Kastner, W.: ThinkHome: a smart home as digital ecosystem. In: IEEE-DEST 2010, pp. 256–261 (2010)
21. Rojo, J., Flores-Martin, D., Garcia-Alonso, J., Murillo, J.M., Berrocal, J.: Automating the interactions among IoT devices using neural networks. In: 2020 IEEE PerCom Workshops, pp. 1–6 (2020). https://doi.org/10.1109/PerComWorkshops48775.2020.9156111
22. Scully, P.: Top 10 IoT applications in 2020, July 2020. https://iot-analytics.com/top-10-iot-applications-in-2020/
23. Shokri, R., Shmatikov, V.: Privacy-preserving deep learning. In: Allerton (2015), pp. 909–910 (2015). https://doi.org/10.1109/ALLERTON.2015.7447103
24. Wang, K., Mathews, R., Kiddon, C., Eichner, H., Beaufays, F., Ramage, D.: Federated evaluation of on-device personalization (2019)
25. Wehmeyer, K.: Assessing users' attachment to their mobile devices, p. 16, August 2007. https://doi.org/10.1109/ICMB.2007.19
26. Yang, T., et al.: Applied federated learning: improving Google keyboard query suggestions (2018)
27. Zhao, Y., Li, M., Lai, L., Suda, N., Civin, D., Chandra, V.: Federated learning with non-IID data (2018)
28. Zhu, A.: Learning From Non-IID data (2020). https://xzhu0027.gitbook.io/blog/ml-system/sys-ml-index/learning-from-non-iid-data

Real-Time Deep Learning-Based Anomaly Detection Approach for Multivariate Data Streams with Apache Flink

Tae Wook Ha, Jung Mo Kang, and Myoung Ho Kim[(⊠)]

Korea Advanced Institute of Science and Technology, Daejeon, Republic of Korea
{twha,jmkang,mhkim}@dbserver.kaist.ac.kr

Abstract. For detecting anomalies which are unexpected behaviors in complex systems, deep learning-based anomaly detection algorithms for multivariate time series have gained a lot of attention recently. While many anomaly detection algorithms have been widely proposed, there has been no work on how to perform these detection algorithms for multivariate data streams with a stream processing framework. To address this issue, we present a real-time deep learning-based anomaly detection approach for multivariate data streams with Apache Flink. We train a LSTM encoder-decoder model to reconstruct a multivariate input sequence and develop a detection algorithm that uses reconstruction error between the input sequence and the reconstructed sequence. We show that our anomaly detection algorithm can provide promising performance on a real-world dataset. Then, we develop a Flink program by implementing three operators which process and transform multivariate data streams in a specific order. The Flink program outputs anomaly detection results in real time, making system experts can easily receive notices of critical issues and resolve the issues by appropriate actions to maintain the health of the systems.

Keywords: Multivariate data streams · Anomaly detection · LSTM encoder-decoder · Stream processing · Apache Flink

1 Introduction

In real-world applications, multivariate data are continuously generated by monitoring complex systems such as readings of sensing devices (e.g. pressure and moisture) in power plants or multiple metrics (e.g. CPU load, network usage) in server machines. Detecting anomalies, unexpected behaviors of the systems, in multivariate data streams is a critical task in managing these systems such that system managers can receive notices of critical issues and resolve the issues by providing appropriate actions to maintain the health of the systems. Traditionally, a system expert defines thresholds of normal behaviors for every measurements and then if a measurement exceeds the defined threshold, it is considered as an anomaly that means the system does not behaves normally. Because the size and complexity of the systems increase, however, the number of sensors

M. Bakaev et al. (Eds.): ICWE 2021 Workshops, CCIS 1508, pp. 39–49, 2022.
https://doi.org/10.1007/978-3-030-92231-3_4

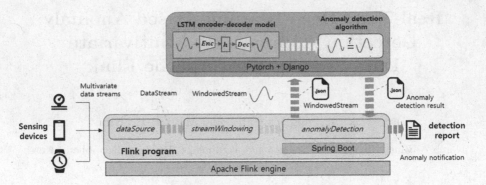

Fig. 1. Overall architecture of an anomaly detection of multivariate data streams with Apache Flink

has dramatically increased making system experts hard to define thresholds of normal behaviors.

To solve this issue, many anomaly detection algorithms have been proposed in multivariate time series data analytic fields for several decades [1]. Several studies [12–14] propose supervised learning methods to detect anomalies, but the lack of labeled anomalous data for model training makes these methods infeasible. As a result, unsupervised anomaly detection methods to learn normal behaviors of the systems have received a lot of attention. Early methods find anomalies by using machine learning models such as k-nearest neighbor [15], clustering [16], one-class svm [17], or a time series prediction model [18]. However, the traditional learning models are not efficient to infer complex dependencies of multivariate time series data. A lot of recent anomaly detection algorithms use deep neural network models such as LSTM encoder-decoder model [2], a deep autoencoder with a Gaussian mixture model [10], LSTM networks with a variational autoencoder [11], LSTM or convolutional LSTM networks for prediction [7,8], bi-directional generative adversarial networks [9] and convolutional recursive encoder-decoder model [3], a stochastic recurrent neural network [4], a temporal hierarchical one-class network [5] and an autoencoder model with adversarial training [6]. While these deep learning-based anomaly detection algorithms have been proposed, as far as we know, there has been no work on how to perform these detection algorithms for multivariate data streams with a stream processing framework.

In this work, we present a real-time deep learning-based anomaly detection approach for multivariate data streams with a stream processing framework, Apache Flink. We first train a LSTM encoder-decoder model in [2] to reconstruct a multivariate sequence and develop an anomaly detection algorithm that uses the reconstruction error between the input sequence and the reconstructed sequence. And then, we develop a Flink program to process multivariate data streams in real time. Flink is one of popular even-driven stream processing frameworks for stateful computations over unbounded data streams. For a user to easily develop a program, Flink provides a programming model that is a directed acyclic graph where each node is an operator that defines a functionality for incoming data streams. With implementing operators, we can specify the order of transformations of the data streams. Figure 1 shows the overall architecture of our Flink program consisting of three operators: *dataSource*, *streamWindowing*, and *anomalyDetection*. *dataSource* operator receives raw data streams and send them to DataStream objects where DataStream is a basic type for handling a data stream in Flink. *streamWindowing* then generates a sequence containing multiple consecutive data from the DataStream object. *anomalyDetection* feeds the sequence into a trained LSTM encoder-decoder model and notifies anomalies by receiving detection results from the detection algorithm.

The rest of this paper is organized as follows. We first discuss an anomaly detection method for a multivariate sequence in Sect. 2. And then we describe implementation details of Flink operators in Sect. 3 and conclude this paper in Sect. 4.

2   Anomaly Detection for a Multivariate Sequence

We focus on a multivariate sequence $X = \{\mathbf{x}_1, \mathbf{x}_2, ..., \mathbf{x}_t, ..., \mathbf{x}_T\}$ of length T where each data point $\mathbf{x}_t \in R^m$ is a m-dimensional vector of readings for m variables at a time step t. Since most real-world applications have lack of labeled anomalous data, we train the LSTM encoder-decoder model with normal sequences obtained by collecting multiple normal sequences or taking a sliding window of length T over a large time series data. After training the LSTM encoder-decoder model, the reconstruction error of each data point in an input sequence is used to compute an anomaly score for the point. A higher anomaly score indicates the point being anomalous, and if the input sequence contains enough anomalous points, we notice that the input sequence is anomaly.

2.1   LSTM Encoder-Decoder Model for Reconstruction

The LSTM encoder-decoder model consists of a LSTM encoder and a LSTM decoder as shown in Fig. 2. Given X, the LSTM encoder updates the hidden state $\mathbf{h}_t^E$ at a time step t for each $t \in \{1, 2, ..., T\}$ where $\mathbf{h}_t^E \in R^d$, d is the number of units in a LSTM network. Note that the final hidden state of the encoder $\mathbf{h}_t^E$ is learnt as a vector representation of X and the LSTM decoder uses $\mathbf{h}_t^E$ as the initial state $\mathbf{h}_t^D$ to reconstruct X in reverse order [2]. A LSTM network in the decoder outputs a reconstructed data point $\mathbf{x}'_t$ at t by computing $\mathbf{x}'_t = \mathbf{W}^\mathbf{T}\mathbf{h}_t^D + \mathbf{b}$ where $\mathbf{W}$ is a weight matrix of a linear layer in the LSTM network and $\mathbf{b} \in R^m$ is a bias vector. Then, $\mathbf{x}'_t$ is used to update the next hidden state $\mathbf{h}_{t-1}^D$. The objective function for model training is $L = \sum_{X \in S_X} \sum_{t=1}^{T} \|\mathbf{x}_t - \mathbf{x}'_t\|^2$ where S_X is a set of normal sequences.

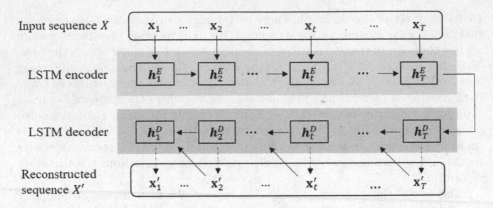

Input sequence X

LSTM encoder

LSTM decoder

Reconstructed
sequence X'

Fig. 2. Inference step of a LSTM encoder-decoder model for an input sequence X to output reconstructed sequence X'

2.2   Computing Anomaly Scores for Detection

Given the input sequence X and the reconstructed sequence X', the output of the LSTM encoder-decoder model, the error vector is obtained by $\mathbf{e}_t = |\mathbf{x}_t - \mathbf{x}'_t|$ for all time steps in X. Then, we compute the anomaly score of each data point $a_t = (\mathbf{e}_t - \boldsymbol{\mu})^T \boldsymbol{\Sigma}^{-1} (\mathbf{e}_t - \boldsymbol{\mu})$ where $\boldsymbol{\mu}$ and $\boldsymbol{\Sigma}$ are a mean vector and a covariance matrix of a normal distribution $\mathcal{N}(\boldsymbol{\mu}, \boldsymbol{\Sigma})$ respectively. $\boldsymbol{\mu}$ and $\boldsymbol{\Sigma}$ are estimated by error vectors $\mathbf{e}_t$ for all data points $\mathbf{x}_t$ in a validation set.

We determine whether the input sequence X is anomaly based on the anomaly scores a_t for all time steps. After we compute an anomaly score a_t at time step t, if $a_t > \tau$, the data point $\mathbf{x}_t$ can be detected as "an anomalous data point", otherwise "a normal data point". If the number of anomalous data points in X is larger than δ, we notice that X is an anomalous sequence. (otherwise, X is noticed by a normal sequence). Note that if there is a very few incorrectly reconstructed data points in X, we consider this is because there are some noises in X making the LSTM encoder-decoder model cannot reconstruct the data points, or a very few anomalies occur but they are not severe to the system [3]. We set the values of τ and δ that maximize $F1 = 2 \times (P \times R)/(P + R)$ score on the validation sequences where P is a precision score and R is a recall score.

2.3   Performance Evaluation of Anomaly Detection

Dataset. To evaluate the performance the anomaly detection described in Sect. 2, we conduct an experiment on a real-world dataset: SMD (Server Machine Dataset). SMD is a new 5-week-long dataset collected by [4] from 28 server machines in a large Internet company. It contains observations measured for every 1 min and each observation has 38 metrics such as TCP active opens, memory usage, CPU load, Disk write, etc. For each machine, data are divided into two subsets of equal size: the first half is a training set and the second half is a testing set. In our experiment, we use 80% of training set for model training and use 20% of training set for model validation. Anomalies in the testing set are labeled by domain experts based on incident reports. Detailed information of SMD dataset can be seen in Table 1. The meanings of columns in Table 1 are as follows. "machine id" is an id of each machine, and "train/validation/test time steps" is the number of observations in the training/validation/testing set. "anomaly time steps" is the number of anomalies in the testing set and "anomaly ratio" is a ratio of anomalies over the testing set. "anomalous periods" is the number of periods of consecutive anomalies.

Table 1. SMD dataset information

Machine id	Train time steps	Validation time steps	Test time steps	Anomaly time steps	Anomaly ratio (%)	Anomalous periods
1-1	22,784	5,695	28,479	2,694	9.46	8
1-2	18,956	4,738	23,694	542	2.29	10
1-3	18,962	4,740	23,703	817	3.45	12
1-4	18,965	4,741	23,707	720	3.04	12
1-5	18,964	4,741	23,706	100	0.42	7
1-6	18,951	4,737	23,689	3,708	15.65	30
1-7	18,958	4,739	23,697	2,398	10.12	13
1-8	18,959	4,739	23,699	763	3.22	20
2-1	18,955	4,738	23,694	1,170	4.94	13
2-2	18,960	4,739	23,700	2,833	11.95	11
2-3	18,951	4,737	23,689	269	1.14	10
2-4	18,952	4,737	23,689	1,694	7.15	20
2-5	18,951	4,737	23,689	980	4.14	21
2-6	22,995	5,748	28,743	424	1.48	8
2-7	18,957	4,739	23,696	417	1.76	20
2-8	18,962	4,740	23,703	161	0.68	1
2-9	22,978	5,744	28,722	1,755	6.11	10
3-1	22,960	5,740	28,700	308	1.07	4
3-2	18,962	4,740	23,693	1,109	4.68	10
3-3	18,963	4,740	28,696	632	2.20	26
3-4	18,950	4,737	23,703	977	4.12	8
3-5	18,952	4,738	23,703	426	1.80	11
3-6	22,981	5,745	23,687	1,194	5.04	11
3-7	22,964	5,741	23,691	434	1.83	5
3-8	22,963	5,740	28,726	1,371	4.77	6
3-9	22,971	5,742	28,705	303	1.06	4
3-10	18,954	4,738	28,704	1,047	3.65	13
3-11	22,956	5,739	28,713	198	0.69	3

Experimental Settings and Evaluation Metrics. We employ Pytorch to implement a LSTM encoder-decoder model for each machine, and train each model on a server with Intel(R) Core(TM) i7-10700k CPU 3.80 GHz, 128 GB memory, and a NVIDIA RTX 3090 graphic card. We empirically set hyper-parameters of the LSTM encoder-decoder model in our experiments as follows. The length of a sliding window, for taking an input sequence, is set to 100 and the overlapping length is set to 10. The number of hidden units in LSTM is fixed to 200. We set the batch size to 5 for model training, and run for 200 epochs with early stopping. We utilize Adam optimizer with a learning rate of 10^{-3} for stochastic gradient descent.

To evaluate the performance of the anomaly detection using LSTM encoder-decoder model, we use three metrics, *i.e.* Precision, Recall, and F1 scores. For an input sequence, it is considered as an anomaly if it contains anomalous data points more than δ. We set the threshold values of τ and δ which maximize the F1 scores over the input sequence taken from the validation set of each machine. Precision and recall scores are then calculated based on these threshold values.

Evaluation Results. Table 2 shows the evaluation results of the anomaly detection algorithm for each machine. With our discussion with experts in some real-world applications, we focus on the high recall scores among the detection results. We can see that the detection algorithm in our work has recall scores higher than 0.90 showing it can be effectively used to detect anomalies in some cases (e.g. 1-1, 1-6, 3-1, 3-4, 3-5, and 3-11). However, we can also see that precision scores lower than 0.1 causing low F1 scores in some machine (e.g. 2-8, 3-5, 3-9, 3-11) because of lack capabilities of the LSTM encoder-decoder model for reconstruction. Thus, this motivated us to improve the performance of the detection algorithm in future work, by searching the optimized hyper-parameters with

Table 2. Performance results on SMD dataset

Machine id	Precision	Recall	F1	Machine id	Precision	Recall	F1
1-1	0.2985	**0.9742**	0.4570	2-7	0.6889	0.2616	0.3792
1-2	0.8269	0.5548	0.6641	2-8	0.0107	0.5769	0.2021
1-3	0.1389	0.6414	0.2284	2-9	0.2790	0.8986	0.4258
1-4	0.1551	0.4974	0.2365	3-1	0.0283	**0.9437**	0.0549
1-5	0.4545	0.6329	0.5291	3-2	0.1291	0.7598	0.2206
1-6	0.3209	**0.9684**	0.4820	3-3	0.4504	0.3814	0.4130
1-7	0.7799	0.7588	0.7692	3-4	0.0833	**0.9943**	0.1536
1-8	0.2864	0.4758	0.3575	3-5	0.0936	**0.9603**	0.1706
2-1	0.6018	0.5407	0.5696	3-6	0.7815	0.8087	0.7949
2-2	0.4511	0.5550	0.4977	3-7	0.0826	0.7128	0.1481
2-3	0.7789	0.5873	0.6697	3-8	0.2756	0.7143	0.3977
2-4	0.2539	0.6230	0.3608	3-9	0.0832	0.8551	0.1517
2-5	0.6602	0.4518	0.5365	3-10	0.2434	0.4681	0.3202
2-6	0.1608	0.8364	0.2698	3-11	0.0504	**0.9773**	0.0959

additional experiments or developing a new model for reconstruction to capture the complex dependencies in multivariate time series data.

3 Implementation Details of Flink Operators

3.1 *dataSource* Operator

dataSource operator reads a raw sensor data and transmit it to the output stream ds. Since our program reads values from multiple sensors, we let ds have a data type <Tuple> containing a sensor id, a value, and a timestamp. We implement our customized source function CustomSrcFunc for reading sensor values by inheriting RichSourceFunction provided by Apache Flink. env gets the environmental information of Flink program and registers the CustomSrcFunc to execute from source s every time interval t. After env calls execution() method to start the program, for every time t, CustomSrcFunc reads a value from s and creates tuple containing an id and a value of s, and a timestamp. Then, tuple is sent to the output stream ds by calling collect() method in ds.

Algorithm 1: *dataSource* operator

---

1 $s \leftarrow$ data source, $t \leftarrow$ time interval
2 ds $\leftarrow$ DataStream<Tuple>
3 CustomSrcFunc $\leftarrow$ RichSourceFunction <Tuple>
4 env $\leftarrow$ getExecutionEnvironment()
5 env.register(CunstomSrcFunc(s, t))

6 **if** env *calls* execution() **then**
7   **while** *every time t* **do**
8   CustomSrcFunc reads a value from s and creates tuple containing an id and a value of s
9   ds.collect(tuple)
10   **end**
11 **end**

3.2 *streamWindowing* Operator

streamingWindowing operator collects multiple tuple from multiple stream ds to build a window with shape $[l, dim]$ and send it to the output stream of windows ws. We first define a parameter value trigger that is the number of tuple to collect and initialize tempwin window by calling createGlobalWindow() method in Apache Flink. When ds collects a tuple, ds puts tuple into tempwin. If the number of tuple in tempwin meets trigger, tempwin calls the sortAggregate() method to sort multiple tuple via timestamps in tuple. After that, tempwin is sent to the output window stream ws by calling collect() method in ws.

3.3   *anomalyDetection* Operator

anomalyDetection operator takes charge of two roles. One is to connect two heterogeneous platforms and the other is to detect anomalous sequences. Our two preceding operators consist of Java but we employ Pytorch to implement a LSTM encoder-decoder model. We need to make it possible to communicate between two different platforms so that we send `tempwin` from `ws` to the LSTM encoder-decoder model for reconstruction. Thus, we adopt a local client-server architecture for communication. We describe the details of our local client-server architecture as follows.

Algorithm 2: *streamWindowing* operator

1 trigger ← *dim* * *l*
2 tempwin ← `createGlobalWindow()`
3 ws ← WindowedDataStream<Tuple>

4 **while** *true* **do**
5   **if** ds *collects* tuple **then**
6   ds puts tuple to tempwin
7   **if** *the numbers of tuples in* tempwin == trigger **then**
8   tempwin ← `tempwin.sortAggregate()`
9   `ws.collect(tempwin)`
10   **end**
11   **end**
12 **end**

The Details of Local Client-Server Architecture. The local client is implemented on a spring boot framework and it behaves asynchronous and event-driven way. On the other hand, the local server is implemented on a Django rest framework. Once receiving `tempwin` from the windowed stream `ws`, the local client makes a JSON file containing the data of `tempwin`. The local client then posts the JSON file to the local server, subscribes to the response from the local server, and waits for the next `tempwin` from `ws`. When the local server receives the JSON file, it calls the `serialize()` to extract `tempwin` in the file. Since `tempwin` already has a tensor of a fixed size (*i.e.*, [*l*, *dim*]), it copies the value of the JSON file to the tensor. The tensor is defined by $Tensor_{in}$ corresponding to the input sequence. The $Tensor_{in}$ is sent to the LSTM encoder-decoder model and the model outputs the reconstructed tensor $Tensor_{re}$. The local server conducts the anomaly detection algorithm to detect anomalies by the procedure of the detection algorithm, as described in Sect. 2.2. After that, `Webserver.create`(*localhost*) calls `response`($result_d$) to response the detection result to `Webclient.create`(*localhost*) which reports the detection result.

Algorithm 3: *anomalyDetection* operator

---

1   $client_{local}$ ← Webclient.create($localhost$)

2   $server_{local}$ ← Webserver.create($localhost$)

3   $client_{local}$ calls post(tempwin)

4   **if** tempwin *is sent* **then**

5     $client_{local}$ subscribes response from $server_{local}$ and waits for the next tempwin from ws

6     $Tensor_{in}$ ← $server_{local}$ calls serialize(tempwin)

7     $Tensor_{re}$ ← LSTM encoder-decoder($Tensor_{in}$)

8   cnt ← 0 to count anomalous data points

9   **forall the** *time step t in length T* **do**

10       $\mathbf{x}_t$ ← $Tensor_{in}$ (t)

11       $\mathbf{x}'_t$ ← $Tensor_{re}$ (t)

12       $e_t = |\mathbf{x}_t - \mathbf{x}'_t|$

13       $a_t = (e_t - \boldsymbol{\mu})^T \boldsymbol{\Sigma}^{-1} (e_t - \boldsymbol{\mu})$

14   **if** $a_t > \tau$ **then**

15   cnt ← cnt +1

16   **end**

17   **end**

18   **if** cnt $> \delta$ **then**

19       $result_d$ ← tempwin is an anomalous sequence

20   **else**

21       $result_d$ ← tempwin is a normal sequence

22   **end**

23     $server_{local}$ calls response($result_d$)

24   **if** $result_d$ *is replied* **then**

25       $client_{local}$ gets $result_d$ and reports $result_d$

26   **end**

27 **end**

---

4   Conclusion

In this paper, we presented a real-time deep learning-based anomaly detection approach of multivariate data streams with Apache Flink. While many deep learning-based anomaly detection algorithms have been proposed in the literature, there has not been no work on how to perform these detection algorithms for multivariate data streams with a stream processing framework. In order to address this issue, we first train a LSTM encoder-decoder model to reconstruct an input sequence and develop a detection algorithm that uses anomaly scores based on errors between the input sequence and the reconstructed sequence. We show that our detection algorithm have promising performance by experimental results on a real-world dataset. Then, we develop a Flink program by implementing three operators which process and transform the multivariate data streams in a specific order. The developed Flink program can provide anomaly notifications in real time, making system experts can easily identify critical issues and maintain the health of the complex systems by providing appropriate solutions.

Acknowledgement. This work was supported by the MSIT (Ministry of Science and ICT), Korea, under the ITRC (Information Technology Research Center) support program (IITP-2020-0-01795) supervised by the IITP (Institute of Information & Communications Technology Planning & Evaluation), and the National Research Foundation of Korea (NRF) grant funded by the Korea government (MSIT) (No. 2020R1A2C1004032).

References

1. Chalapathy, R., Chawla, S.: Deep learning for anomaly detection: a survey. arXiv preprint arXiv:1901.03407 (2019)
2. Malhotra, P., et al.: LSTM-based encoder-decoder for multi-sensor anomaly detection. arXiv preprint arXiv:1607.00148 (2016)
3. Zhang, C., et al.: A deep neural network for unsupervised anomaly detection and diagnosis in multivariate time series data. In: Proceedings of the AAAI Conference on Artificial Intelligence, vol. 33, no. 01 (2019)
4. Su, Y., et al.: Robust anomaly detection for multivariate time series through stochastic recurrent neural network. In: Proceedings of the 25th ACM SIGKDD International Conference on Knowledge Discovery and Data Mining (2019)
5. Shen, L., Li, Z., Kwok, J.: Timeseries anomaly detection using temporal hierarchical one-class network. In: Advances in Neural Information Processing Systems, vol. 33 (2020)
6. Audibert, J., et al.: USAD: unsupervised anomaly detection on multivariate time series. In: Proceedings of the 26th ACM SIGKDD International Conference on Knowledge Discovery and Data Mining (2020)
7. Hundman, K., et al.: Detecting spacecraft anomalies using LSTMs and nonparametric dynamic thresholding. In: Proceedings of the 24th ACM SIGKDD International Conference on Knowledge Discovery and Data Mining (2018)
8. Tariq, S., et al.: Detecting anomalies in space using multivariate convolutional LSTM with mixtures of probabilistic PCA. In: Proceedings of the 25th ACM SIGKDD International Conference on Knowledge Discovery and Data Mining (2019)
9. Zenati, H., et al.: Adversarially learned anomaly detection. In: 2018 IEEE International Conference on Data Mining (ICDM). IEEE (2018)
10. Zong, B., et al.: Deep autoencoding gaussian mixture model for unsupervised anomaly detection. In: International Conference on Learning Representations (2018)
11. Park, D., Hoshi, Y., Kemp, C.C.: A multimodal anomaly detector for robot-assisted feeding using an LSTM-Based variational autoencoder. IEEE Robot. Autom. Lett. **3**(3), 1544–1551 (2018)
12. Park, D., et al.: A multimodal execution monitor with anomaly classification for robot-assisted feeding. In: 2017 IEEE/RSJ International Conference on Intelligent Robots and Systems (IROS). IEEE (2017)
13. Rodriguez, A., et al.: Failure detection in assembly: force signature analysis. In: 2010 IEEE International Conference on Automation Science and Engineering. IEEE (2010)
14. Görnitz, N., et al.: Toward supervised anomaly detection. J. Artif. Intell. Res. **46**, 235–262 (2013)

15. Hautamaki, V., Karkkainen, I., Franti, P.: Outlier detection using k-nearest neighbour graph. In: Proceedings of the 17th International Conference on Pattern Recognition. ICPR 2004, vol. 3. IEEE (2004)
16. He, Z., Xiaofei, X., Deng, S.: Discovering cluster-based local outliers. Pattern Recogn. Lett. **24**(9–10), 1641–1650 (2003)
17. Manevitz, L.M., Yousef, M.: One-class SVMs for document classification. J. Mach. Learn. Res. **2**, 139–154 (2001)
18. Brockwell, P.J., Davis, R.A., Fienberg, S.E.: Time Series: Theory and Methods. SSS. Springer Science & Business Media, New York (1991). https://doi.org/10.1007/978-1-4419-0320-4

A Novel Approach to Dynamic Pricing for Cloud Computing Through Price Band Prediction

Dheeraj Rane[✉] [iD], Vaishali Chourey[iD], and Ishan Indraniya[iD]

Medi-Caps University, Indore, India
{dheeraj.rane,vaishali,en18cs301106}@medicaps.ac.in

Abstract. Cloud computing emerges as a boon to business enterprises that offers increased productivity, economic efficiency and least operational and maintenance costs. The cost for the services offered is variable and dependent on market trends. The pricing model for cloud services are pay-per-use or subscription based as required circumstantially. With more and more provisions created for growing demands of resources, the pricing models are metering the requirements and are constantly moderating to provide optimal prices for services yet keeping best revenue schemes. To deliver business value to customers with QoS considerations within limits of infrastructure that they have, a price-wise categorization is required. In addition to this, the operational cost as well as infrastructure cost for cloud providers will differ insignificantly based-on whether one consumer or multiple consumers are serviced. The subscription model to service provisioning by the provider end is fueled up with discounts, price-cuts, offers and benefits to lure the customers thereby maximizing their resource utilization implicitly. Therefore, in order to grab the opportunity created by this competitive environment, we propose a dynamic pricing model for cloud brokers. In the existing cases of unexpected costs due to resource constraints going towards higher extremities, our model evaluates a price band for the customer's transparency in cost and optimizes it. The benefits of the proposed pricing model is two fold. It provides the assurance about the maximum price that will be charged to the consumer while enjoying the existing benefits of dynamic pricing model; the price range calculation is an estimation done on the basis of resources requested, price history, current price, and risk premium are the decisive factors for our estimation rule. A fair proposition of resource allocation with maximal resource utilization, due returns for investments and an effective cost offering for the services is the aim of our work.

Keywords: Cloud computing · Dynamic pricing · Pricing analysis

1 Introduction

In the cloud computing environment, as there are n number of cloud service providers it is difficult to determine from which provider a specific cloud service

© Springer Nature Switzerland AG 2022
M. Bakaev et al. (Eds.): ICWE 2021 Workshops, CCIS 1508, pp. 50–61, 2022.
https://doi.org/10.1007/978-3-030-92231-3_5

should be availed. At present, different providers list their offerings in different manner. As there is no standardized way to list the offerings, the decision to choose one among many seems challenging. Even if the decision about the provider is being made, second decision to be made is regarding which of their offerings is appropriate based on the requirement. Third, many times situations may arise to combine services of multiple cloud service providers to achieve some functionality, or the consumer may need the existing service in an enhanced manner. Therefore, to address all the above concerns the concept of cloud service broker arises. Cloud service broker facilitates intermediation, aggregation and arbitration of cloud services offered by different cloud providers.

A pricing model is required to make a decision about the price of cloud service based on analytics by considering a host of factors such as reference prices, cost prices, sales prices, forecasts, expected demand, market intent and bulk acquisition costs to arrive at a set of actionable insights. While arriving at these insights is one side of a coin, determining what insights to go with is another. An intelligent pricing model takes into account more than market intuitions. It considers the degree of demand, supply and product/service scope as parameters before determining the price. Therefore, it's imperative for cloud service brokers, regardless of their scale to adopt a holistic intelligent pricing solution that customarily aligns itself to the company and the market dynamics it faces to profit cloud service consumers. At broad level pricing can be fixed or dynamic. Fixed pricing refers to traditional approach where price is fixed for a service or resource. It can be charged on per hour basis or for the tenure it is availed. While, in case of dynamic pricing, pricing of resource varies time to time based on the demand of the service or resource.

By all this, it is clear that pricing is very crucial in the concept of cloud computing. Pricing is at the core of the concept of cloud computing. The importance towards pricing is because the notion of accessing computing needs as and when required, without owning them only by paying for used resources, is the foundation of cloud computing [8]. In addition to this, attractive offerings extended by Cloud Service Providers (CSPs) such as Amazon spot instances may result in up to 90% reduction in Amazon Elastic Compute Cloud (EC2) instance price. Based on the suggestions of spot bid advisor the savings range from 63% to 91% for different instances of Amazon EC2. The attempt of the cloud computing industry should lie around this notion whether the resources required are for few hours or for a long time. In this quest, efforts are made to introduce a pricing model for cloud broker, which is dynamic in nature.

In this work, we attempt to define a dynamic pricing model for cloud broker where the idea is to introduce a pricing scheme in which instead of fixed pricing, the broker will provide a price range to the consumer. This price range will have a minimum price and maximum price, which denotes the lower bound and upper bound of the amount that can be charged to the consumer respectively. So, the charged price will always be within this range. The proposed algorithm for pricing variation makes a consistent effort so that the average price should remain lower than fixed price for the same set of resources.

This paper is organized as follows. The next section describes the pricing model for cloud brokering architecture is presented. Further, Sect. 3, put forward an evaluation of proposed pricing model. Next, Sect. 4 provides the details about related work. Section 5 concludes the paper.

2   Cloud Broker Pricing Model

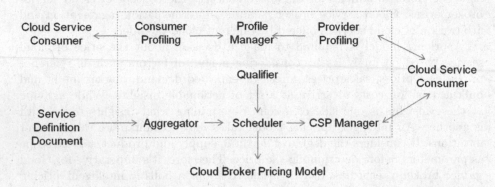

Fig. 1. Cloud broker pricing model. A dynamic pricing model that offers price band.

For obtaining best solution and pricing, a cloud broker offering dynamic pricing can prove to be a viable solution. However, the risk of fluctuation in dynamic pricing cannot be ignored. This means if a consumer relies on dynamic pricing to take the benefits of market fluctuation and suddenly the price get hiked due to massive demand then the consumer will have to bear a considerable loss. Some capping is therefore required at both ends i.e. lower bound and upper bound as well. This delimitation will ensure provider about a minimum amount that will be received and at the same time will assure a consumer about the limit beyond which the hired resource will not be charged. Accordingly, we have proposed Dynamic Pricing Algorithm for Cloud Brokering (DPA-CB), a pricing model for cloud broker (Fig. 1). DPA-CB aims at introducing a pricing band to cloud consumer in order to assure the consumer about the minimum and maximum rates that will be charged corresponding to requested resources. Once cloud consumer agrees to the contract, cloud broker will manage the allocation of computing resources to appropriate cloud provider based on the requirements and constraints placed by cloud consumer. The allocation to the provider will be transparent to the consumer; however, the control will not be there with the consumer to select a particular cloud provider.

Providers are also there as a component of DPA-CB, so as to publicize their computing resources. A unique id is assigned to the computing resources listed by a provider. Here, the price of resources need to be maintained by the cloud provider, and hence, the provider may increase or reduce the price based on the demand and availability of resources. After this, the resources are ready to be assigned to the cloud consumers if they suffice consumer's resource requirements.

DPA-CB then executes an algorithm to assign the listed resources to the cloud consumers, which as an output gives an allocation matrix having the resources and corresponding cloud consumer. Cloud broker then shares the unique id of the resource with the consumer, using which consumer gets the access to the resource. The DPA-CB system is compatible with the prominent cloud providers such as Amazon EC2, Google Compute Engine and Microsoft Azure and hence the proposed model can easily be deployed with Virtual Machines (VMs) of these service providers.

Apart from the algorithm that will decide on the allocation of a provider's resource to a consumer, DPA-CB also provides a user interface (UI) that can be used by the cloud provider and cloud consumer as well. Authentication mechanisms are incorporated to verify the identity of providers and consumers. Cloud providers can enlist their resources with a proper description along with the price. On the other hand, cloud consumers can use the DPA-CB interface to specify required resources, non-functional requirements, duration and basic Service Level Agreement (SLA) requirements. DPA-CB logs the allocation details and performance parameters, which will help the providers and consumers to track the allocation history, accounting details, current allocations, request status, SLA compliance and usage statistics. Hence, in DPA-CB we have tried to find an assignment that fulfills the requirement of the consumer in a best possible manner as per the situation.

2.1   Basic Model

The goal of DPA-CB is to facilitate allocation of services offered by the cloud provider to a cloud consumer in a manner, so as to optimize the total cost borne by cloud consumer. For this, a pricing band is offered to cloud consumer having lower and upper limits within which the resource will be charged. Therefore, to get a final optimized price, reallocation should be done as and when required.

This work introduces a pricing model (Fig. 1) composed of modules such as *demand-supply monitoring, consumer profile, quality class, historical pricing, pricing band calculator* and *subscription module*.

As specified, the idea of the pricing model is to propose a pricing band to the cloud consumer corresponding to resources requested. Later, the pricing model will make a consistent effort to optimize the price charged by grabbing the opportunity raised by other providers and then migrating to these provider resources. Therefore, assuming P_{vl} and P_{vh} be the lower limit and upper limit of the variable pricing band offered to consumer c for the resource set R (Fig. 3). Further, assuming P_{ij} be the price charged from a consumer i by the provider j, where a consumer i utilized the resources of m different providers during the contract period (Fig. 2). Then the price charged by a consumer i can be given by (1)

$$P_a = \sum_{j=1}^{m} P_{ij} \tag{1}$$

Algorithm 1: MIGRATIONDECISION determines the possibility of migration

---

Input: Finite sets C, Q, D, S and H of integers
Output: Migrates resources to other cloud provider if found favorable

```
1  while True do
2  │   if trigger condition is true then
3  │   │   for every consumer c∈C having condition triggered do
4  │   │   │   m ← re-execute allocation algorithm
5  │   │   │   p ← calc_migration(m)
6  │   │   │   d ← compare(p, e)
7  │   │   │   if d < 1 then
8  │   │   │   │   migrate
9  │   │   │   else
10 │   │   │   │   continue
11 │   │
12 │
```

On the other side, let P_f be the fixed price charged by the provider j, if consumer i preferred fixed pricing instead of variable pricing. Provider j is the preferable provider at time t_0 i.e. the time when contract period started. So, under such circumstances the objective of DPA-CB will be to make consistent effort to achieve the following relation (2):

$$P_a < P_f \tag{2}$$

Therefore, the lower limit and the upper limit defined by DPA-CB can be assumed as follows:

$$P_{vl} = P_f - c_1$$
$$P_{vh} = P_f + c_2 \tag{3}$$

Here, c_1, c_2 denotes the marginal cost needed to maintain the limits. In few situations, c_1 can have same value as c_2.

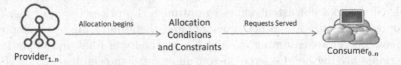

Allocation begins   Allocation   Requests Served
                       Conditions
                       and Constraints
Provider$_{1..n}$ Consumer$_{0..n}$

Fig. 2. Dynamic pricing. Price band is offered that gives minimum and maximum price that will be charged.

2.2   Pricing Band Estimation

Cloud resources are demanded over time by different cloud consumers through cloud resource broker. Cloud resource broker offers a price band to the consumer

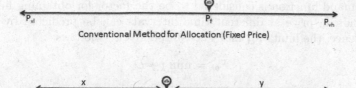

Proposed Method for Allocation

Fig. 3. Pricing limits. Gives a comparison with conventional models and average price charged is less than fixed price.

for the resources requested. Pricing band ensures that the charged price will be within the limits and not beyond. On acceptance, cloud broker makes continuous efforts to bring the average price below the fixed price. This is done by grabbing new offerings from providers and migrating the VMs to them.

Let, T be the time for which the consumer have requested the resource k and is given by:

$$T \leftarrow \{t_s, t_{s+1}, \ldots\ldots, t_{s+d}\} \tag{4}$$

While offering pricing band, the cloud resource broker emphasizes on dynamic pricing. The dynamism in price offered by cloud service provider will be taken as an advantage to reduce the pricing charged over required duration. According to [3] the relation between price and demand with respect to time using following stochastic demand function:

$$D(t, p, \xi) \tag{5}$$

In Eq. [5], ξ is the margin of error. Further, with demand function D it is assumed that this function returns the demand determined by price. This demand is used as the factor to multiply with the price and then to determine the final price.

In case of static pricing, as the price is fixed for the complete duration of the contract, the price should be optimized only once. Corresponding to time t, user category u and quality class q, following optimization problem can be solved to optimize the price for static pricing model:

$$maximize \sum_{t=1}^{T} \sum_{u=1}^{U} \sum_{q=1}^{Q} (D(t, p, \xi)) \tag{6}$$

While for dynamic pricing, the price may change even after allocation of the resources. Therefore, apart from the time, there can be several other factors that will affect the price, and hence the demand function needs to be modified. Hence, utilizing the variables of function f described in Equation [6] the demand function can be written as:

$$D(n, t, q, c, r, h) \tag{7}$$

As the demand function is considered to be the factor for obtaining final price, the variation in price at different time intervals can be predicted by utilizing Eq. [7]. Hence, the limits P_{vl} and P_{vh} can be given as follows:

$$P_{vl} = \min_{\forall t \in T} p * D_t$$
$$P_{vh} = \max_{\forall t \in T} p * D_t \tag{8}$$

Now, cloud resource broker will offer these limits to the consumer and for the whole contract period, the price charged to the consumer will range in between the limits. The broker will gain profit in case some provider offers resources below P_{vl}. On the other side, the consumer will be benefited if the dynamic pricing goes beyond P_{vh}. Here, efforts are made to anticipate the boundary in which the dynamic pricing may fluctuate and not on maximizing the revenue of cloud resource broker.

3 Evaluation

In this section, the experimental setup for the proposed pricing model is described. The experimentation is primarily aimed at evaluating the practicality of the pricing model DPA-CB. A prototype is developed to support the evaluation process. Primarily, the prototype consists of two important modules: *Price band calculator module* and *VM manager module*. Price band calculator module is responsible for calculating the price band corresponding to the consumer's requirements while VM manager module corresponds to deployment agent. For the simulation of price band calculator module, the time duration for demand analysis is considered to be ten days. Demand factor is calculated using demand function and by utilizing this demand factor the values of P_{vl} and P_{vh} are observed (Table 2). Different requirements will lead to different values of demand factor at different time instances. For example, only after changing the duration of historical data, the change in demand factor can be seen as described in column 3) of Table 1. The range for the factor of demand analysis is taken from 0.2 to 3.0. The assumption made here is that the demand can be as low as 20% of the demand at time t_s i.e. the start time, and it can go up to 300% on the other side.

Further, for actual values of price change corresponding to the period for which the values of P_{vl} and P_{vh} are calculated, Amazon EC2 spot pricing is utilized. The pricing considered is for 60 d on Linux/UNIX machine with t1. Micro configuration situated in us-east-1c region. For the whole tenure under consideration, the price ranged from \$0.003/hr to \$0.005/hr.

However, the same instance of Amazon EC2, if considered for fixed price would have cost \$0.013/hr. A comparison of dynamic pricing when limits are offered and that of fixed pricing is given in Fig. 4.

It can be observed that dynamic pricing model DPA-CB performs extraordinarily well in the scenario considered. Particularly, it proves to be a win-win situation for both providers as well as the consumer. For example, considering

Table 1. Values of demand factor

Time (Days) (1)	Demand factor (D)	
	Historical data (Last 60 days) (2)	Historical data (Last 30 days) (3)
Start	1	1
10	1.47	0.82
20	0.22	1.27
30	1.28	0.76
40	0.75	0.7
50	0.67	1.11
60	0.9	0.62

Table 2. Limits assigned for different demand factor

Demand factor (Last 60 days)		Demand factor (Last 30 days)	
P_{vl}	P_{vh}	P_{vl}	P_{vh}
0.0026	0.02	0.009	0.016

the case of demand factor when last 30 days historical data was considered the lower limit came out to be $0.009. This means that at least $0.009 will be charged irrespective of the price charged by the provider. As the spot price charged for the observed duration range from $0.003 to $0.005, so broker is getting a considerable margin per hour. On the other side, it is assured that the maximum price charged in any circumstances is $0.016 per hour. This safeguards a consumer against sudden surge such as [6], where Amazon EC2 spot request volatility hits $1000/hr. Further, Fig. 5 shows the percentage gain by adoption of DPA-CB and it can be observed that as the number of days are increasing the performance of DPA-CB is improving.

With this elementary evaluation, it can be observed that the idea of proposing a pricing band instead of relying merely on dynamic pricing is favorable for all the stakeholders participating in the cloud market.

4   Related Work

As cloud computing is a promising technology [10] and is still said to be in evolving state [14] , so new ventures concerning providers are regularly emerging. Also, because of its competitive environment, existing companies keep on announcing attractive offerings time-to-time. However, sticking to fixed pricing scheme in such evolving and competitive market, will limit the consumer from availing the benefits of these conditions. Hence, use of dynamic pricing will help to conform to the continually changing market. It facilitates maximum revenue generation by properly adjusting price with respect to demand and appropriate utilization

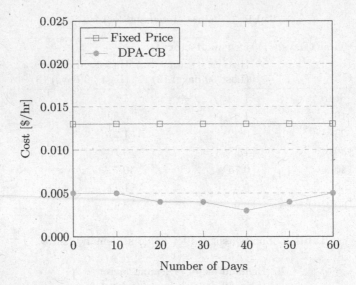

Fig. 4. Effective pricing at different instances (Color figure online)

of resources. Currently, most of the cloud service providers have adapted fixed pricing scheme [7] except Amazon spot pricing [1]. Providers with fixed pricing scheme promote allocation strategies such as on-demand and reserved instances, while Amazon provides spot instances as well, along with the other two. However, spot instance resources can anytime be interrupted and claimed back by Amazon, resulting in loss of work if the application running is not able to handle the interrupt.

Cloud pricing schemes are mainly classified as fixed pricing scheme, dynamic pricing scheme, and hybrid pricing. Among these, fixed pricing scheme is one adapted by default and is always compared with all other approaches. Therefore, related work on cloud pricing schemes is mainly focused on Hybrid pricing. Again, as cloud computing concept is still evolving, the description is prepared with pricing schemes pertaining to Grid and Web Services. This description is followed by consideration of existing work on cloud pricing schemes.

4.1   Hybrid Pricing

The hybrid pricing model makes an attempt to provide a diversified model that incorporate advantages of both fixed price model and pay-per-use model. This way, the hybrid pricing model utilizes fixed pricing in normal conditions and maximizes benefits by executing tasks through pay-per-use as and when some good offering arrives. Hybrid pricing model proves best for massive and lengthy projects with unsettled objectives in the beginning. Apart from several benefits for the consumer, it also gives the cloud service provider a more controlled infrastructure with shared liability in financial terms.

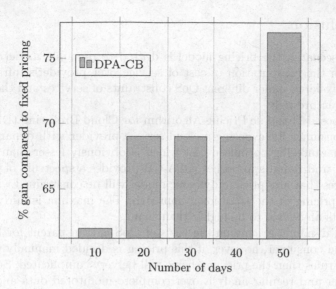

Fig. 5. Percentage gain by adoption of DPA-CB

For information services, the hybrid pricing model is presented as two-part tariff pricing in [13], that examines the optimality of the pricing scheme that should be adopted by a provider in different conditions. The considerations done for making the decision about a particular pricing is on the basis of consumer behavior, as whether the consumers are homogeneous consumers or heterogeneous consumers. Further, the sensitivity of optimal pricing scheme is analyzed with respect to marginal costs and monitoring costs. Overall, efforts are made to help provider to choose best pricing model on the basis of consumer type (homogeneous or heterogeneous) and the trend between marginal and monitoring cost.

Huang et al. [9] looked hybrid pricing scheme with another aspect where the authors examined the effectiveness of hybrid pricing model for a cloud service provider where fixed pricing scheme is mixed with spot-instance pricing. The difference introduced here is its look-out towards cloud service as damaged perspective, where spot-instances can be claimed any time through an interrupt. The decision support model proposed in this work helps a cloud provider to decide whether the hybrid pricing scheme is suitable or not. Yet another study done in [4] proves that hybrid pricing model is more efficient than subscription pricing and pay-per-use pricing as well.

Other related systems that help cloud service consumer to obtain a comparison of cloud providers on the basis of various factors including pricing model adapted are [2, 5, 11, 12].

To the best of our knowledge, the proposed approach does not match with any of the existing work. However, we have utilized the basic concept of dynamic pricing.

5   Conclusion

In current scenario, the pricing model is drifted to dynamic model to provide flexibility in the computation of cost of service over provider's infrastructure. Services are offered under different QoS constraints of services and therefore the prices vary accordingly.

We proposed Dynamic Pricing Algorithm for Cloud Brokering (DPA-CB) to facilitate consumer for choosing a cloud service provider with dynamic pricing and also guaranteeing optimized cost which is obviously lesser than the prices available in traditional approaches. DPA-CB provides a spectrum of price band which assures that any price in dynamic model will be constrained within lower to average pricing of the traditional approach. The maxima is fairly proposed that restricts any value to be higher than that.

Further, dynamic pricing on the basis of QoS is transparent for both cloud provider and consumer, however, if this pricing is decided manually or through pre-defined rules then the pricing scheme will be very complicated. Such pricing needs proper and regular analysis over complete monitored data and weighing of some features to seek importance of one feature over another. Therefore, as future work a machine learning approach can be developed having the capability to continuously analyze a large amount of data through big data analytics and hence making optimized pricing decisions.

There are few situations in which DPA-CB may not be useful as expected. In the case of a very frequent change in demand for a computing resource, the system will indulge into the consistent migration of VMs, yielding no work but still paying the cost of migration. As a consequence, the system performance will also downgrade, where the system is greedy and decides to migrate to optimize the total cost. Further, there are issues in migration that needs to be handled. Therefore, as further research in cloud broker pricing model, authors recommend modeling a robust pricing model, capable enough to manage the frequent fluctuations in demand. Further, the behavior of inseparability of computing resources may lead to utility functions producing sub-optimal assignment. Measures should be taken in future work to address this issue as well.

References

1. Agmon Ben-Yehuda, O., Ben-Yehuda, M., Schuster, A., Tsafrir, D.: Deconstructing Amazon EC2 spot instance pricing. ACM Trans. Econ. Comput. **1**(3), 1–20 (2013)
2. Amazon: Amazon EC2 spot cloud (2016). http://spotcloud.com/. Accessed 18 Jan 2016
3. Bitran, G., Caldentey, R.: An overview of pricing models for revenue management. Manuf. Serv. Oper. Manag. **5**(3), 203–229 (2003)
4. Chun, S., Sam Choi, B., Woong Ko, Y., Hak Hwang, S.: Frontier and Innovation in Future Computing and Communications, chapter The Comparison of Pricing Schemes for Cloud Services, pp. 853–861. Springer, Netherlands (2014)
5. Cloudorado. Cloudorado: Cloud computing comparison engine (2015). https://www.cloudorado.com/. Accessed 03 Nov 2015

6. Amazon EC2: Amazon EC2 spot request volatility (2016). https://moz.com/devblog/amazon-ec2-spot-request-volatility-hits-1000hour/. Accessed 19 Jan 2016
7. Sharma, B., et al.: Pricing cloud compute commodities: a novel financial economic model. In: Proceedings of the 2012 12th IEEE/ACM International Symposium on Cluster, Cloud and Grid Computing (CCGrid 2012), pp 451–457. IEEE Computer Society, Washington, DC, USA (2012)
8. Fox, A.: Above the clouds: a Berkeley view of cloud computing. In: Department Electrical Engineering and Computer Sciences, University of California, Berkeley, Report UCB/EECS, 2009-28 (2009)
9. Huang, J., Kauffman, R.J., Ma, D.: Pricing strategy for cloud computing: a damaged services perspective. Decis. Sup. Syst. **78**, 80–92 (2015)
10. Mell, P., Grance, T.: The NIST definition of cloud computing (2011)
11. Misc: Smart cloud broker (2015). http://www.smartcloudbroker.com/. Accessed 03 Nov 2015
12. PlanForCloud. Planforcloud: Cloud portfolio management (2015). https://www.planforcloud.com/. Accessed 03 Nov 2015
13. Wu, S.Y., Banker, R.: Best pricing strategy for information services. J. Assoc. Inf. Syst., **11**(6), 339–366 (2010)
14. Yousif, M.: A plethora of challenges and opportunities. IEEE Cloud Comput. **1**(2), 7–12 (2014)

Learning-Based Activation of Energy Harvesting Sensors for Fresh Data Acquisition

Sinwoong Yun[1], Dongsun Kim[1], and Jemin Lee[2]([✉])

[1] Daegu Gyeongbuk Institute of Science and Technology, Daegu 42988, South Korea
{lion4656,yidaever}@dgist.ac.kr
[2] Sungkyunkwan University, Suwon 16419, South Korea
jemin.lee@skku.edu

Abstract. We consider an energy harvesting wireless sensor network (EH-WSN), where each sensor, equipped with the battery, senses its surrounding area. We first define the estimation error of the sensing data at a measuring point, which increases as the distance to the sensor increases and the age of information (AoI) of the data increases. The AoI is the elapsed time since the latest status is generated. We also define the network coverage, which is defined as the area having the estimation errors lower than a target value. As a performance metric, we use the α-coverage probability, which is the probability that the network coverage is larger than a threshold α. Finally, in order to deal with dynamic and complex environments, we propose a reinforcement learning (RL) based algorithm which determines the activation of the sensors. In simulation results, we show the proposed algorithm achieves higher performance than baselines. In addition, we show the impact of the transmission power and the number of sensors on the α-coverage probability.

Keywords: Age of information · Energy harvesting wireless sensor network · Reinforcement learning

1 Introduction

A wireless sensor network (WSN) introduces the energy harvesting at the sensors to reduce the maintenance cost from battery replacement [7]. There are some works on energy harvesting wireless sensor network (EH-WSN)s [2,8,9], which try to improve the energy efficiency by scheduling the sensor activation. However, the sensing coverage models in those works do not take into account the freshness of sensing data which can affect the reliability of sensing information.

The data freshness is a metric that quantifies a timeliness of the information [4]. An age of information (AoI) has been introduced as a measurement of data freshness, which is defined as the elapsed time of the data from its generation. Although some recent works try to consider the AoI at sensor network, they do not address the sensor activation strategy in AoI-affected coverage model.

© Springer Nature Switzerland AG 2022
M. Bakaev et al. (Eds.): ICWE 2021 Workshops, CCIS 1508, pp. 62–68, 2022.
https://doi.org/10.1007/978-3-030-92231-3_6

Motivated from this, we consider the sensor activation for the data freshness in EH-WSN. First, we newly define an estimation error that is affected by the AoI and the distance between the sensor and the measured point. We then define the α-coverage probability, which is the probability that the portion of the area having the lower estimation error than the certain threshold α. By adopting the recent deep reinforcement learning (RL) technique, we develop the intelligent sensor activation algorithm to maximize the α-coverage probability under the battery and energy-harvesting constraints. From the simulation results, we show the proposed method outperforms other baselines. Furthermore, we show the impacts of transmission power and the number of sensors on the α-coverage probability.

2   Proposed Model

2.1   Network Description

We consider an EH-WSN, which consists of multiple sensors and a sink node. Each sensor collects information about its surrounding environment and transmits the sensing data to the sink node. Due to the limited battery, sensors should be charged by harvesting the energy. For each discrete time slot, the sensor takes one of the following operations: sensing, transmission, and harvesting.

The energy level of the n-th sensor at the time slot t is given as

$$B_n[t] = \min\left(B_n[t-1] + e_n[t], B^{max}\right), \tag{1}$$

where B^{max} denotes the maximum capacity of battery, and $e_n[t]$ denotes the energy consumption or gain determined by operation of the sensor. Note that sensing and transmission consume a certain amount of energy $(e_n[t] < 0)$ and cannot be taken at insufficient energy level, while harvesting yields an energy that follows exponential distribution $(e_n[t] > 0)$.

The success of the transmission is determined by the signal-to-noise ratio (SNR) at the sink node. Then the successful transmission probability (STP) can be defined as the probability that SNR exceeds a certain threshold. Generally, in noise-limited wireless transmission, STP increases as the transmission power increases and the distance between the transmitter and the receiver decreases. If the sensor fails to transmit data and has sufficient energy, it can retransmit the data to the sink node. When the battery level is insufficient to transmit the data, it harvests energy until it has sufficient energy for transmission.

2.2   Problem Formulation

AoI in EH-WSN. Figure 1 shows the AoI in n-th sensor over time. The AoI can be defined in terms of AoI at the sensor and the sink node, of which each is represented by $\Delta_n^{tx}[t]$ and $\Delta_n^{rx}[t]$, respectively.

The AoI at the sensor, i.e., $\Delta_n^{tx}[t]$, is the time since the sensor performs sensing. When the sensor performs sensing at time t, $\Delta_n^{tx}[t] = 1$. Otherwise, $\Delta_n^{tx}[t]$ increases linearly, i.e., $\Delta_n^{tx}[t] = \Delta_n^{tx}[t-1] + 1$.

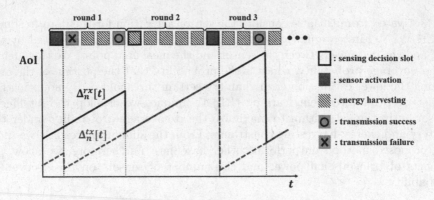

Fig. 1. AoI at the sensor and the sink node.

The AoI at the sink node, i.e., $\Delta_n^{rx}[t]$, is defined as the time gap from the time the sensor performs sensing to the time the sink node obtains the information. When the transmission succeeds at time t, $\Delta_n^{rx}[t] = \Delta_n^{tx}[t-1] + 1$. Otherwise, $\Delta_n^{rx}[t]$ increases linearly, i.e., $\Delta_n^{rx}[t] = \Delta_n^{rx}[t-1] + 1$.

AoI-Affected Sensing Coverage. The generated information at the point is spatio-temporally correlated. It means that an estimation error of the information at a measuring point can be higher as the distance between the point and the sensor is larger or the time after sensing is longer. As in [3], we consider the observed information as a stationary Gaussian process, and the estimation error for the n-th sensor for the point at (x, y) is defined as

$$\epsilon_n^{(x,y)}[t] = 1 - \exp\left(-2\beta_1 d_n^{(x,y)} - 2\beta_2 \Delta_n^{rx}[t]\right), \tag{2}$$

where $d_n^{(x,y)}$ is a distance between n-th sensor and the point with location (x, y) and β_1 and β_2 are the weights of the spatial error and temporal error, respectively. The information at the point can be obtained by nearby sensors, and the sink node may use the information of the point which has the minimum estimation error. Note that we assume the sink node can obtain the information of the sensors such as the location and the AoI at the sensor.

The information is reliable when the estimation error is smaller than the threshold ϵ_0. Then, the AoI threshold at the point (x, y) to be in the coverage of n-th sensor can be expressed by the function of $d_n^{(x,y)}$ as

$$\Delta_{th}\left(d_n^{(x,y)}\right) = \frac{-2\beta_1 d_n^{(x,y)} - \ln(1 - \epsilon_0)}{2\beta_2}. \tag{3}$$

The sink node can only exploit the information where $\Delta_n^{rx}[t]$ does not violate the AoI threshold $\Delta_{th}\left(d_n^{(x,y)}\right)$. Therefore, the sensing coverage of n-th sensor shrinks as $\Delta_n^{rx}[t]$ increases. On the other side, the sensing coverage expands when the sensor successfully transmits the data packet to the sink node.

A network coverage refers to the ratio of areas covered by one or more sensors in the interested region. In our proposed model, it is equivalent to the area having the estimation errors lower than a target value. It can be thought that the information in the network can be reliable when the overall network coverage satisfies a certain ratio. Therefore, we adopt α-coverage probability, the probability that the network coverage satisfies α or more, as a performance metric.

2.3 Proposed Algorithm

Generally, it is hard to get the optimal solution, especially for the complex and dynamic environments. Therefore, we propose the deep RL-based algorithm to learn the sensing decision policy to maximize the α-coverage probability. First, we describe the α-coverage probability maximization problem using Markov Decision Process (MDP).

1) Agent: an agent takes action based on the current state. In this problem, the sink node acts as the agent and determines the joint activation of the sensors at each sensing decision slot. The goal of the agent is to maximize expected cumulative reward.
2) State: state at the beginning of each round contains information about a) battery level of the sensors $B_n[t]$, b) AoI at the sensor sides $\Delta_n^{tx}[t]$, c) AoI at the sink node sides $\Delta_n^{rx}[t]$.
3) Action: using state as input, the agent outputs the action through a deep neural network. The sink node decides whether each sensor performs sensing or not at sensing decision slot. Sensors with low battery level cannot perform sensing, so the action set changes at every sensing decision slot.
4) Reward: the objective of the problem is to maximize the α-coverage probability. However, it is difficult to calculate the probability in an episodic environment. Instead, we set the reward as the sum of an event whether the network coverage is not less than α during at each round, given as

$$r = \sum_{t=\tau}^{\tau+T_r} \left(\mathbb{1}[\phi_{cov}[t] \geq \alpha] - \mathbb{1}[\phi_{cov}[t] < \alpha] \right), \qquad (4)$$

where τ is the first time slot at current round, T_r is the number of time slots at each round and $\phi_{cov}[t]$ is the overall network coverage at t.

In RL, the agent learns a policy on what action to take for the given state. In spite of the same problem, learning performance varies significantly with the type of algorithm and hyperparameters. One of the famous algorithms is Deep Deterministic Policy Gradient (DDPG), a policy gradient based RL algorithm that can be operated over a continuous action space to address the curse of dimensionality [5].

However, training performance of DDPG may not be sufficient for the environment where 1) the reward is inconsistent in the same state-action pair 2) or

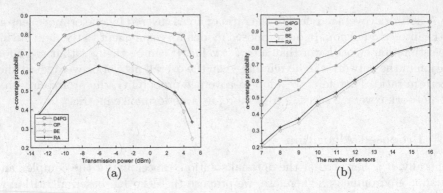

Fig. 2. (a) Impact of transmission power on the α-coverage probability. (b) Impact of the number of sensors on the α-coverage probability.

the temporal correlation gives a significant impact. Recently, combining a number of enhancements with traditional DDPG, Distributed Distributional Deep Deterministic Policy Gradient (D4PG) algorithm has improved the performance on physical control tasks [1]. D4PG has some additional properties such as distributional critic, K-step return and prioritized experience replay. We can achieve higher performance compared to DDPG by adopting the D4PG to solve the proposed problem.

3   Simulation Results

Simulation results are carried out by using Tensorflow 2.1.0 to evaluate the performance of proposed algorithm compared with following baselines:

1) Greedy policy (GP): Sensor is activated if its battery level is higher than or equal to sum of sensing and transmission energy, which is used in [6].
2) Best effort (BE): Sensor having sufficient battery for sensing is activated.
3) Random activation (RA): Sensor is activated with half probability. If the battery level of the sensor is lower than sensing energy, it will not be activated.

Figure 2(a) shows the α-coverage probability with different transmission power for the 7 sensors in the network. We first observe that the proposed D4PG based algorithm outperforms other baselines. We can also see that the α-coverage probability first increases and then decreases as the transmission power increases. When the transmission power is small, as the transmission power increases, the fresh information can be maintained, since the probability of having retransmission decreases. However, above a certain point, the performance decreases with the transmission power because the transmission energy consumption increases, and the energy required for sensing or transmission may be depleted thereafter. Additionally, we observe the impact of the number of sensors in the irregular sensor deployment scenario. Figure 2(b) shows the α-coverage probability as a function of the number of the sensors at 0 dBm transmission. From this figure, we can see that the α-coverage probability increases as the number of sensors increases over all schemes. This is because if more sensors are activated, the probability that each point can transmit fresh information to the sink node increases. Alternatively, it is possible to increase the energy efficiency by becoming idle state while an adjacent sensor performs sensing. Definitely, the α-coverage probability converges to 1 as the number of sensors increases.

4   Conclusion

In this paper, we design the novel sensor activation algorithm for the data freshness in EH-WSN. We first define the AoI at the sensor and the sink node in EH-WSN. Next, we obtain the AoI threshold, which is a function of distance between the sensor and the measuring point, for ensuring that the estimation error does not exceed the error threshold. Then we formulate the α-coverage probability maximization problem reflecting the sensing coverage that changes according to the AoI at the sink node. Finally, we describe the discrete time MDP for the α-coverage probability maximization problem and adopt the recent RL algorithm to obtain the activation policy.

In the simulation results, we first show the proposed sensor activation algorithm outperforms the other baselines. Then, we observe the impacts of the transmission power and the number of sensors on the α-coverage probability. Specifically, as the transmission power of the sensors increases, the α-coverage probability first increases and then decreases, since both the STP and the transmission energy consumption increases with the transmission power. Furthermore, the α-coverage probability increases gradually as the number of sensors increases due to the more activated sensors and the energy efficiency.

References

1. Barth-Maron, G., et al.: Distributed distributional deterministic policy gradients. In: Int. Conf. on Learning Representations (ICLR), Vancouver, Canada, April 2018
2. Chen, H., Li, X., Zhao, F.: A reinforcement learning-based sleep scheduling algorithm for desired area coverage in solar-powered wireless sensor networks. IEEE Sens. J. **16**(8), 2763–2774 (2016)
3. Hribar, J., Costa, M., Kaminski, N., DaSilva, L.A.: Using correlated information to extend device lifetime. IEEE Internet Things J. **6**(2), 2439–2448 (2018)
4. Kaul, S., Yates, R., Gruteser, M.: Real-time status: How often should one update? In: Proceedings IEEE Conference on Computer Communications, pp. 2731–2735, FL, USA, March 2012
5. Lillicrap, T.P., et al.: Continuous control with deep reinforcement learning. In: International Conference on Learning Representations (ICLR), San Juan, Puerto Rico, May 2016
6. Liu, W., Zhou, X., Durrani, S., Mehrpouyan, H., Blostein, S.D.: Energy harvesting wireless sensor networks: delay analysis considering energy costs of sensing and transmission. IEEE Trans. Wirel. Commun **15**(7), 4635–4650 (2016)

7. Shaikh, F.K., Zeadally, S.: Energy harvesting in wireless sensor networks: a comprehensive review. Renew. Sustain. Energy Rev. **55**, 1041–1054 (2016)
8. Yang, C., Chin, K.W.: Novel algorithms for complete targets coverage in energy harvesting wireless sensor networks. IEEE Commun. Lett. **18**(1), 118–121 (2013)
9. Zheng, J., Cai, Y., Shen, X., Zheng, Z., Yang, W.: Green energy optimization in energy harvesting wireless sensor networks. IEEE Commun. Mag. **53**(11), 150–157 (2015)

Invited Papers

Exploiting Triangle Patterns for Heterogeneous Graph Attention Network

Eunjeong Yi[1] and Min-Soo Kim[2(✉)]

[1] DGIST, Daegu, Republic of Korea
`iej0710@dgist.ac.kr`
[2] KAIST, Daejeon, Republic of Korea
`minsoo.k@kaist.ac.kr`

Abstract. Recently, graph neural networks (GNNs) have been improved under the influence of various deep learning techniques, such as attention, autoencoders, and recurrent networks. However, real-world graphs may have multiple types of vertices and edges, such as graphs of social networks, citation networks, and e-commerce data. In these cases, most GNNs that consider a homogeneous graph as input data are not suitable because they ignore the heterogeneity. Meta-path-based methods have been researched to capture both heterogeneity and structural information of heterogeneous graphs. As a meta-path is a type of graph pattern, we extend the use of meta-paths to exploit graph patterns. In this study, we propose TP-HAN, a heterogeneous graph attention network for exploiting triangle patterns. In the experiments using DBLP and IMDB, we show that TP-HAN outperforms the state-of-the-art heterogeneous graph attention network.

Keywords: Graph neural networks · Heterogeneous graph · Triangle

1 Introduction

Recently, graph neural networks (GNNs) have received attention in deep learning over graphs. Many techniques that have been successful in deep learning have also been applied to GNNs. For example, [1,6] proposed the neighbor aggregation method, which was the basis of the graph convolution operation. Veličković et al. [2] proposed an attention mechanism that enabled the neural network to learn which neighbors were important. Chiang et al. [8] proposed a mini-batch algorithm based on graph clustering to reduce the memory and computational requirements for processing large-scale graphs.

Most studies on GNNs considered homogeneous graphs. In contrast, real-world data, such as citation networks and protein–protein interaction networks, are heterogeneous graphs with multiple types of vertices and edges. Therefore, a naïve approach is to ignore heterogeneity of vertices and edges and regard the graph as homogeneous. However, this approach ignores the properties of

M. Bakaev et al. (Eds.): ICWE 2021 Workshops, CCIS 1508, pp. 71–81, 2022.
https://doi.org/10.1007/978-3-030-92231-3_7

heterogeneous graphs, and a method exploiting these properties is required. Recently, methods that use meta-paths have been proposed to consider the heterogeneity. Wang et al. [4] transformed a heterogeneous graph into homogeneous by manually selecting meta-paths and applying the attention mechanism [2]. This method operates by extracted homogeneous graphs for each meta-path, and thus it can have worse performance depending on the selected meta-paths. Yun et al. [5] transformed a heterogeneous graph into useful meta-path-based graphs by automatically generating meta-paths. As the number of stacked layers determines the maximum length of the generated meta-paths, it requires heavy computation to generate long meta-paths. In addition, because it learns to generate useful meta-paths as combinations of edge types, performance can be affected by more edge types.

We focus on meta-paths as a type of a graph pattern. Our approach leverages graph patterns instead of meta-paths to solve the above limits of meta-path-based methods. As a starting point of our approach, we propose TP-HAN, a heterogeneous graph attention network that exploits triangle patterns. TP-HAN improves the performance by exploiting triangle patterns compared with the heterogeneous graph attention network [4] called HAN. In our experiments, we evaluated the performance of TP-HAN by comparing it with that of HAN.

2   Preliminaries

2.1   Heterogeneous Graph

A heterogeneous graph is a graph that has multiple types of vertices and edges. As shown in Fig. 1(a), an academic graph includes three types of vertices—author (A), paper (P), and conference (C)—and multiple types of edges, such as relations between authors and papers, papers and conferences, and pairs of papers.

Table 1. Notations

Notation	Description
Φ	Meta-path
T	Triangle
P	Pattern
X	Vertex feature
A_t	Adjacency matrix for type t
$N_{v_i}^p$	Pattern type p based neighbors of vertex v_i
$\alpha_{v_i v_j}^{\Phi}$	Vertex-level attention of the vertex pair (v_i, v_j) for meta-path Φ
β_v^{Φ}	Semantic-level attention of vertex v for meta-path Φ
$h_{v_i}^{\Phi}$	Vertex-level embedding of vertex v_i for meta-path Φ
W	Parameters of neural network
Z	Final embedding

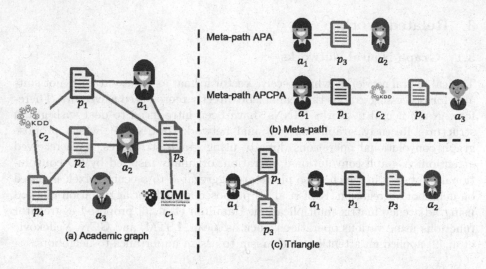

Fig. 1. Example of an academic graph. (a) Heterogeneous graph with three types of vertices (i.e., author, paper, and conference) and three types of edges (i.e., author–paper, paper–conference, and paper–paper relations). (b) Examples of two types of meta-paths (i.e., author–paper–author and author–paper–conference–paper–author). (c) Examples of triangles.

2.2 Meta-Path

Meta-path [3], which is a composite relation of multiple relations, is a widely used structure to capture the semantic information of a heterogeneous graph. Figure 1(b) shows two examples of meta-paths: author–paper–author (A-P-A) and author–paper–conference–paper–author (A-P-C-P-A). For example, two authors, a_1 and a_2, are connected via paper p_3 at meta-path A-P-A. Two authors a_1 and a_3 are connected via paper p_1, a conference c_2, and a paper p_3 on meta-path A-P-C-P-A.

2.3 Triangle

Graph pattern is a frequently seen subgraph. Triangle is a basic and important pattern in graph systems because it is a cycle and also the minimal clique. Therefore, triangle counting and listing are widely used in graph systems. As shown in Fig. 1(c), there are two examples of triangles. For example, author a_1, paper p_1, and paper p_3 form a triangle. In addition, the other triangle, which is formed by author a_1, paper p_1, paper p_3, and author a_2, appears only in a heterogeneous graph. This type of triangle starts at a vertex and arrives at another vertex of the same type via two different vertices. These two types of triangles appear because of heterogeneity of the graph.

3   Related Work

3.1   Graph Neural Networks

Typical neural networks, which receive vector format as input data, are not suitable for processing graphs that cannot be directly represented as vectors. Therefore, graph neural networks (GNNs) have been introduced to deal with graph structure. Recently, graph convolutional networks (GCNs) [1], which propose graph convolutional operations directly using graph structures, have received attention. A graph convolutional operation, originally inspired by 2D convolutional operation in which close pixels are aggregated to a center pixel, is based on neighbor aggregation. Kipf et al. [1] proposed a neighbor aggregation method using adjacency matrix multiplication. Hamilton et al. [6] proposed aggregator functions using various operations, such as mean, LSTM, and GCN. Veličković et al. [2] applied an attention mechanism to assign importance to neighbors.

3.2   Meta-path-Based Graph Neural Networks

Many studies on GNNs assume that the input graph is homogeneous, but such methods are not suitable for processing heterogeneous graphs. Instead, meta-path-based GNNs have been proposed to process heterogeneous graphs.

Wang et al. [4] proposed a hierarchical attention mechanism that consists of vertex-level attention and semantic-level attention. Vertex-level attention assigns different importance to neighbors in the extracted homogeneous graph from the heterogeneous graph. Semantic-level attention assigns different importance to each meta-path. Figure 2 shows the overall process of HAN for author a_2 that uses meta-paths A-P-A and A-P-C-P-A.

First, homogeneous graphs are extracted from input graph for each meta-path. A path from author a_2 to author a_1 via paper p_3 corresponds to meta-path A-P-A. Therefore, author a_2 is connected with author a_1 in the graph based on meta-path A-P-A. Likewise, there are some paths matching meta-path A-P-C-P-A. For example, author a_2 is connected with author a_1 because there is a path from author a_2 to author a_1 via paper p_2, conference c_2, and paper p_1. HAN calculates the vertex-level attention between author a_1 and each neighbor in the extracted graph for each meta-path. For meta-path A-P-A, author a_1 is aggregated to author a_2 with importance $\alpha_{a_2a_1}^{\Phi_{APA}}$. In addition, authors a_1 and a_3 are aggregated to author a_2 with importances $\alpha_{a_2a_1}^{\Phi_{APCPA}}$ and $\alpha_{a_2a_3}^{\Phi_{APCPA}}$ for meta-path A-P-C-P-A. After aggregating neighbors with vertex-level attention, HAN calculates the semantic-level attention of meta-paths A-P-A and A-P-C-P-A. The final embedding of a_2 is generated by aggregating the vertex-level embedding $h_{a_2}^{\Phi_{APA}}$ and $h_{a_2}^{\Phi_{APCPA}}$ with the semantic-level attention $\beta_{a_2}^{\Phi_{APA}}$ and $\beta_{a_2}^{\Phi_{APA}}$, respectively. Because HAN uses homogeneous graphs extracted based on meta-paths, it requires manually selected meta-paths. If manual meta-paths are selected incorrectly, HAN can have worse performance.

Yun et al. [5] proposed graph transformer networks (GTNs) that automatically generated possible meta-paths using the edge type for learning to produce

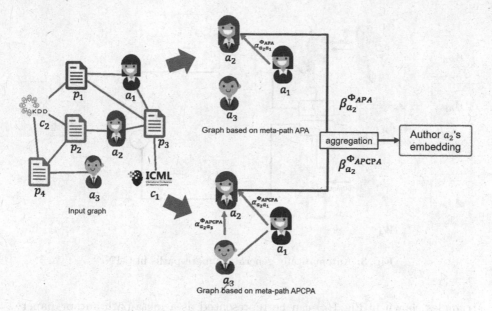

Fig. 2. Overall process of HAN.

useful meta-paths. The GTN generates meta-paths by multiplying an adjacency matrix of an edge type with an adjacency matrix of another edge type. Figure 3 shows the process of automatically generating meta-paths. As shown in Fig. 3, there are four types of edges: paper–author (P-A), author–paper (A-P), paper–conference (P-C), and conference–paper (C-P). To select two edge types, the GTN conducts a softmax operation for parameters W_1 and W_2. In Fig. 3, the edge types A-P and P-C are selected in the green boxes of the results of softmax operation for parameters W_1 and W_2, respectively. The GTN obtains an adjacency matrix A_{APC} of meta-path A-P-C by multiplying an adjacency matrix A_{AP} with an adjacency matrix A_{PC}. The number of generated meta-paths is determined by the channel of the parameter. For example, in Fig. 3, the GTN generates three types of meta-paths with parameters W_1 and W_2 ($W_1, W_2 \in \mathbf{R}^{4 \times 3}$) that have three channels. When the number of stacked layers is increased, the length of the generated meta-path is increased by one. If there are many edge types, the number of possible meta-paths increases exponentially. Selecting a few meta-paths among a number of possible meta-paths can lead to performance degradation. In addition, because meta-paths are generated by matrix multiplication, heavy computation may be required to generate various meta-paths or long meta-paths.

4 TP-HAN: Exploiting Triangle Patterns

We focus on the fact that meta-path is a type of graph pattern. Graph patterns that are the Eulerian path can be represented as meta paths. For example, the

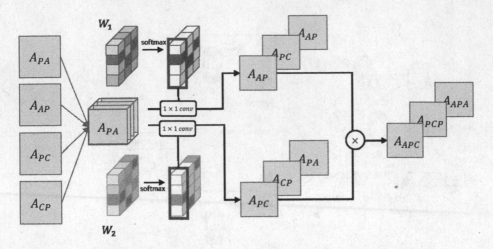

Fig. 3. Automatically generating meta-paths in GTN.

triangles shown in Fig. 1(c) can be represented as a meta-path author–paper–paper–author (A-P-P-A). However, more complex graph patterns, such as a kite pattern and a clique, cannot be represented as meta-paths or can only be represented as long meta-paths. Therefore, we expect that using graph patterns can capture graph structures that are difficult to represent using meta-paths. We propose a heterogeneous graph attention network exploiting triangle patterns, called TP-HAN, as a starting point of the hypothesis that using graph patterns leads to performance improvement of GNNs.

Figure 4, shows the process of extracting a homogeneous graph using a triangle A-P-P-A. Subgraphs that are matched to triangle A-P-P-A are extracted. A homogeneous graph is extracted by considering that two vertices on a triangle are connected. For example, there is a triangle that includes author a_1, paper p_1, p_3, and author a_2. Authors a_1 and a_2 are connected to the extracted homogeneous graph for the author vertices.

Algorithm 1 shows the pseudo code of our TP-HAN. In lines 1–6, TP-HAN extracts triangle-based homogeneous graphs. The adjacency matrices for triangles are calculated by multiplying the adjacency matrices of the edge types that form a triangle. For example, for triangle A-P-P-A, there are three edge types: A-P, P-P, and P-A. From a set $E_{APPA} = \{t_{AP}, t_{PP}, t_{PA}\}$, TP-HAN obtains an adjacency matrix A_{APPA} by multiplying $A_{t_{AP}}$, $A_{t_{PP}}$, and $A_{t_{PP}}$. Likewise, in lines 7–12, TP-HAN extracts the meta-path-based homogeneous graphs. For each pattern p_r, TP-HAN calculates the vertex-level attention between vertices v_i and v_j and aggregates neighbors $N_{v_i}^{p_r}$. TP-HAN adopts a multihead attention mechanism [2], which consists of K independent attentions. Line 11 represents concatenation of each vertex-level embedding for each attention head. In line 13, TP-HAN calculates semantic-level attention for each pattern p_r. TP-HAN generates the final embedding Z by aggregating the semantic embedding h^{p_r} with semantic-level attention β^{p_r}.

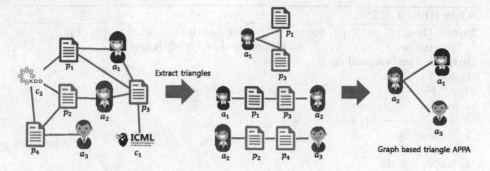

Fig. 4. Extracting triangle-based graphs.

5 Experiment

5.1 Datasets

To evaluate the effect of using triangles, we extracted the subsets of DBLP[1] and IMDB[2]. The detailed statistics of the heterogeneous graphs are presented in Table 2. Figure 5 shows the triangles used in DBLP and IMDB. We find the triangles using adjacency matrix multiplications.

Table 2. Data statistics.

Dataset	$|V|$			$|E|$			Feature	Training	Validation	Test
DBLP	A	4,805	20,049	P-A	7,442	33,382	6,823	800	400	3,605
	P	15,226		P-P	10,714					
	C	18		P-C	15,226					
IMDB	M	11,237	31,091	M-M	2,458	31,775	4,467	900	900	9,437
	A	17,401		M-A	25,314					
	D	2,453		M-D	4,003					

DBLP contains three types of vertices (papers (P), authors (A), and conferences (C)) and three types of edges (paper–author (P-A), paper–paper (P-P), and paper–conference (P-C)). Labels denote the research area of authors. Author features are represented by the bag-of-words of paper abstracts. Manual metapaths are A-P-A and A-P-C-P-A, which were also selected in [4]. In Fig. 5(a), there is a triangle A-P-P-A in DBLP.

---

[1] https://dblp.uni-trier.de/.
[2] https://www.imdb.com/.

Algorithm 1. TP-HAN

Input: Graph $G = (V, E)$, feature X, label Y, meta-path set $\Phi = \{\Phi_1, \Phi_2, \ldots, \Phi_m\}$,
triangle set $T = \{T_1, T_2, \ldots, T_n\}$, number of attention heads K
Output: Final embedding Z
1: **for** $T_i \in T$ **do**
2:     $E_{T_i} \leftarrow \{t_j | t_j$ is an edge type forming a triangle $T_i\}$
3:     **for** $t_j \in E_{T_i}$ **do**
4:         $A_{T_i} \leftarrow A_{T_i} \cdot A_{t_j}$
5:     **end for**
6: **end for**
7: **for** $\Phi_i \in \Phi$ **do**
8:     $E_{\Phi_i} \leftarrow \{t_j | t_j$ is an edge type forming a meta-path $\Phi_i\}$
9:     **for** $t_j \in E_{\Phi_i}$ **do**
10:         $A_{\Phi_i} \leftarrow A_{\Phi_i} \cdot A_{t_j}$
11:     **end for**
12: **end for**
13: $P \leftarrow A_\Phi \cup A_T$
14: **for** $p_r \in P$ **do**
15:     **for** $k = 1, \ldots, K$ **do**
16:         **for** $v_i \in V$ **do**
17:             Find the pattern-based neighbors $N_{v_i}^{pr}$;
18:             **for** $v_j \in N_{v_i}^{pr}$ **do**
19:                 Calculate the vertex-level attention $\alpha_{v_i v_j}^{pr}$;
20:             **end for**
21:             Calculate the vertex-level embedding $h_{v_i}^{pr} \leftarrow \sigma(\Sigma_{j \in N_{v_i}^{pr}} \alpha_{v_i v_j}^{pr} \cdot X_{v_j})$;
22:         **end for**
23:         Concatenate the vertex-level embedding from all attention heads
                $h_{v_i}^{pr} \leftarrow \|_{k=1}^{K} h_{v_i}^{pr}$;
24:     **end for**
25:     Calculate the semantic-level attention β^{pr};
26:     Fuse the semantic embedding $Z \leftarrow \Sigma_{i=1}^{m+n}(\beta^{p_i} \cdot h^{p_i})$;
27: **end for**
28: Calculate cross-entropy $L = -\Sigma_{l \in Y} Y_l \log(Z_l)$;
29: Calculate gradients $g \leftarrow \Delta L$;
30: Update parameters W;
31: **return** Z

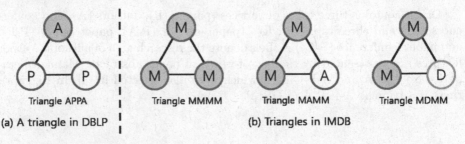

Fig. 5. Utilized triangles. (a) Triangle pattern in the DBLP. (b) Three types of triangle patterns in IMDB (i.e., movie–actor–movie–movie (M-A-M-M), movie–director–movie–movie (M-D-M-M), and movie–movie–movie–movie (M-M-M-M)).

The Internet Movie Database (IMDB) contains three types of vertices (movies (M), actors (A), and directors (D)) and three types of edges (movie–movie (M-M), movie–actor (M-A), and movie–director (M-D)). Labels denote the genres of movies. Movie features are represented by the bag-of-words of plots. Manual meta-paths are M-A-M, M-D-M, and M-M-M. Meta-paths M-A-M and M-D-M were also selected in [4]. Figure 5(b) shows three types of triangles: M-M-M-M, M-A-M-M, and M-D-M-M.

5.2 Experimental Settings

We experimentally compare TP-HAN with HAN. For the experiment, we used a machine with a 40-core 2.2 GHz Intel Xeon CPU, 512 GB of main memory, and a Tesla V100 GPU. For both HAN and TP-HAN, we set the learning rate to 0.005, the number of attention heads to 8, the dropout to 0.6, the regularization parameter to 0.001, and the dimension of the semantic-level attention vector to 128. The model was optimized by Adam [7] optimizer.

5.3 Finding Meta-Paths and Triangles

Figure 5 shows the used triangle types for DBLP and IMDB. We extracted the triangle-based homogeneous graphs using adjacency matrix multiplications. Moreover, we measured the elapsed time for finding subgraphs, which were matched to meta-paths and triangles, and counted their number. In Table 3, the most frequent subgraph of DBLP is a meta-path A-P-C-P-A, which requires longer time to compute than other meta-paths. In IMDB, the most frequent subgraph is a triangle M-M-M-M, and the pattern that requires the longest time to compute is a triangle M-A-M-M.

5.4 Vertex Classification

TP-HAN exploits both meta-paths used in HAN and the triangle patterns. We measure both the macro F1 and the micro F1 for vertex classification to compare performance according to the presence of a triangle. Table 4 presents the macro F1 and the micro F1 for the vertex classification. In Table 4, TP-HAN that uses both meta-paths and a triangle outperforms HAN that uses only manual meta-paths. This result shows that using a triangle improves the performance of HANs.

Table 3. Elapsed time and the number of meta-paths and triangles

Dataset	Pattern type		Number of patterns	Elapsed time (s)
DBLP	Meta-path	A-P-A	11,176	0.0023
		A-P-C-P-A	4,983,312	0.6452
	Triangle	A-P-P-A	3,351	0.0027
IMDB	Meta-path	M-M-M	18,552	0.0018
		M-A-M	95,628	0.0074
		M-D-M	20,203	0.0025
	Triangle	M-M-M-M	134,364	0.0037
		M-A-M-M	46,130	0.0093
		M-D-M-M	9,105	0.0033

Table 4. Results of the vertex classification task

Dataset	Metrics	HAN	TP-HAN
DBLP	Macro F1	0.954	**0.962**
	Micro F1	0.968	**0.973**
IMDB	Macro F1	0.498	**0.504**
	Micro F1	0.557	**0.561**

We compare the performance of TP-HAN by varying the number and type of triangle patterns used for TP-HAN with the meta-paths as a default. Table 5 presents both the macro F1 and the micro F1 for the vertex classification depending on the number and type of used triangle patterns. In Table 5, TP-HAN with two triangles, M-D-M-M and M-M-M-M, achieves the best performance for the micro F1 compared to the others. In addition, TP-HAN exploiting a triangle M-D-M-M obtains better performance in terms of the macro F1 than the others. Moreover, regardless of the number and type of used triangle patterns, TP-HAN

Table 5. Results depending on the number of triangle patterns in IMDB

Method	Utilized triangle pattern		Metrics	
			Macro F1	Micro F1
HAN	Only meta-path	M-A-M, M-D-M, M-M-M	0.498	0.557
TP-HAN	A triangle	M-A-M-M	0.504	0.565
		M-D-M-M	**0.505**	0.568
		M-M-M-M	0.503	0.563
	Two triangles	M-A-M-M, M-D-M-M	0.504	0.564
		M-A-M-M, M-M-M-M	0.500	0.559
		M-D-M-M, M-M-M-M	0.504	**0.576**
	All triangles	M-A-M-M, M-D-M-M, M-M-M-M	0.504	0.561

consistently shows better performance than HAN. These results indicate that TP-HAN outperforms HAN by exploiting triangle patterns.

6 Discussion and Future Work

In this study, we proposed TP-HAN, a heterogeneous graph attention network that exploits triangle patterns. According to our results, TP-HAN improved performance in terms of accuracy compared to HAN. We verified that exploiting triangle patterns is better than using only meta-paths.

We expect that exploiting graph patterns, which are frequently seen and are more complex than a triangle, improves the performance of GNNs. Therefore, the development of GNNs that exploit graph patterns is expected to have the potential to be addressed in future work. This direction is expected to overcome problems such as high computational cost and the requirement of manual meta-paths.

Acknowledgement. This research was supported by the MSIT (Ministry of Science and ICT), Korea, under the ITRC (Information Technology Research Center) support program (IITP-2021-2020-0-01795) supervised by the IITP (Institute of Information & Communications Technology Planning & Evaluation).

References

1. Kipf, T.N., Welling, M.: Semi-supervised classification with graph convolutional networks. In: The International Conference on Learning Representations (2017)
2. Veličković, P., Cucurull, G., Casanova, A., Romero, A., Lio, P., Bengio, Y.: Graph attention networks. In: The International Conference on Learning Representations (2018)
3. Dong, Y., Chawla, N.V., Swami, A.: Metapath2vec: scalable representation learning for heterogeneous networks. In: Proceedings of the 23rd ACM SIGKDD International Conference on Knowledge Discovery and Data Mining, pp. 135–144 (2017)
4. Wang, X., et al. : Heterogeneous graph attention network. In: The World Wide Web Conference, pp. 2022–2032 (2019). https://doi.org/10.1145/3308558.3313562
5. Yun, S., Jeong, M., Kim, R., Kang, J., Kim, H.J.: Graph transformer networks. In: Advances in Neural Information Processing Systems, vol. 32, pp. 11983–11993 (2019)
6. Hamilton, W.L., Ying, R., Leskovec, J.: Inductive representation learning on large graphs. In: Proceedings of the 31st International Conference on Neural Information Processing Systems, pp. 1025–1035 (2017)
7. Diederik P.K., Jimmy B.: Adam: a method for stochastic optimization. In: The International Conference on Learning Representations (2015)
8. Chiang, W.L., Liu, X., Si, S., Li, Y., Bengio, S., Hsieh, C.J.: Cluster-GCN: an efficient algorithm for training deep and large graph convolutional networks. In: Proceedings of the 25rd ACM SIGKDD International Conference on Knowledge Discovery and Data Mining, pp. 257–266 (2019)

Towards Seamless IoT Device-Edge-Cloud Continuum: Software Architecture Options of IoT Devices Revisited

Antero Taivalsaari[1,2], Tommi Mikkonen[3,4], and Cesare Pautasso[5(✉)]

[1] Nokia Bell Labs, Tampere, Finland
antero.taivalsaari@nokia-bell-labs.com
[2] Tampere University, Tampere, Finland
[3] University of Helsinki, Helsinki, Finland
tommi.j.mikkonen@jyu.fi
[4] University of Jyväskylä, Jyväskylä, Finland
[5] Università della Svizzera Italiana (USI), Lugano, Switzerland
c.pautasso@ieee.org

Abstract. In this paper we revisit a taxonomy of client-side IoT software architectures that we presented a few years ago. We note that the emergence of inexpensive AI/ML hardware and new communication technologies are broadening the architectural options for IoT devices even further. These options can have a significant impact on the overall end-to-end architecture and topology of IoT systems, e.g., in determining how much computation can be performed on the edge of the network. We study the implications of the IoT device architecture choices in light of the new observations, as well as make some new predictions about future directions. Additionally, we make a case for isomorphic IoT systems in which development complexity is alleviated with consistent use of technologies across the entire stack, providing a seamless continuum from edge devices all the way to the cloud.

Keywords: Internet of Things · IoT · Embedded devices · Programmable world · Software architecture · Software engineering · Edge computing · Isomorphism · Isomorphic software · Liquid software

1 Introduction

The Internet of Things (IoT) represents the next significant step in the evolution of the Internet. The emergence of the Internet of Things will bring us connected devices that are an integral part of the physical world. We believe that this evolution will ultimately result in the creation of a *Programmable World* in which even the simplest and most ordinary everyday things and artifacts in our surroundings are connected to the Internet and can be accessed and programmed remotely. The possibility to connect, manage, configure and dynamically reprogram remote devices through local, edge and global cloud environments will open up a broad variety of new use cases, services, applications and device categories, and enable entirely new product and application ecosystems [1,2].

© Springer Nature Switzerland AG 2022
M. Bakaev et al. (Eds.): ICWE 2021 Workshops, CCIS 1508, pp. 82–98, 2022.
https://doi.org/10.1007/978-3-030-92231-3_8

From economic perspective, the Internet of Things represents one of the most significant growth opportunities for the IT industry in the coming years. According to Fortune Business Insights, the global Internet of Things market size stood at USD 250.72 billion in 2019, and is projected to reach USD 1463.19 billion (nearly $1.5 trillion) by 2027, exhibiting a CAGR of 24.9% during the forecast period[1].

At the technical level, the Internet of Things is all about *turning physical objects and everyday things into digital data products and services* – bringing new value and intelligence to previously lifeless things. Effectively this means adding computing capabilities and cloud connectivity to hitherto unconnected devices, as well as adding backend services and web and/or mobile applications for viewing and analyzing data and controlling those devices in order to bring new value and convenience to the users. Given the integrated, connected nature of the devices, applications and cloud, IoT systems are *end-to-end* (E2E) systems in which the visible parts – the devices and the apps – are only a small part of the overall solution.

In our earlier work, we have pointed out that a common, generic end-to-end (E2E) architecture for IoT systems has already emerged. Furthermore, we have also identified relevant research topics and problems associated with IoT development [3–5]. In this paper we will revisit those topics, and analyze the software architecture options for IoT devices in view of new occurrences in the industry in the past four years. We study the implications of the IoT device architecture choices in light of the new occurrences, as well as make some new predictions about future directions. More specifically, we make a case for isomorphic IoT systems in which development complexity is alleviated with consistent use of technologies across the entire end-to-end system, spanning from IoT/mobile devices on the edge all the way to the cloud. The paper is based on the authors' experiences in a number of industrial and academic IoT development projects carried out in the past ten years, as well as countless discussions with our colleagues and acquaintances in the academia and in the industry.

The structure of this paper is as follows. In Sect. 2, we start the paper by discussing the generic end-to-end IoT system architecture that serves as the backdrop for the rest of the paper. In Sect. 3, we examine the basic software architecture options for IoT devices. In Sect. 4, we focus on the emergence of inexpensive AI/ML hardware, which is bringing significant changes in the overall IoT system architecture by enabling much more computationally intensive AI/ML capabilities at the edge of the IoT systems. In Sect. 5, we make a case for isomorphic IoT software technologies that will be crucial in driving the industry towards a more seamless device-edge-cloud technology continuum. We discuss the implications of these trends briefly in Sect. 6. Finally, in Sect. 7 we draw some conclusions.

---

[1] https://www.fortunebusinessinsights.com/industry-reports/internet-of-things-iot-market-100307.

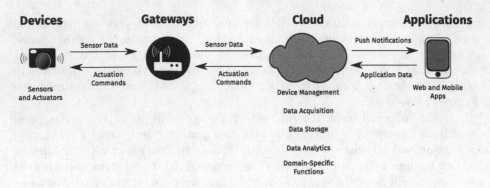

Fig. 1. Conventional generic end-to-end (E2E) IoT architecture.

2   Background

Given the connected nature of smart things and the need for a backend service, IoT systems are *end-to-end* (E2E) systems that consist of a number of high-level architectural elements that tend to be pretty much identical in all IoT solutions. In our 2018 IEEE Software article, we pointed out that a common, generic end-to-end (E2E) architecture for IoT systems has already emerged [3].

As depicted in Fig. 1, IoT systems generally consist of Devices, Gateways, Cloud and Applications. *Devices* are the physical hardware elements that collect sensor data and may perform actuation. *Gateways* collect, preprocess and transfer sensor data from devices, and may deliver actuation requests from the cloud to devices. *Cloud* has a number of· important roles, including data acquisition, data storage and query support, real-time and/or offline data analytics, device management and device actuation control. *Applications* range from simple web-based data visualization dashboards to highly domain-specific web and mobile apps. Furthermore, some kind of an administrative web user interface is typically needed, e.g., for managing usage rights and permissions. Granted, IoT product offerings have their differentiating features and services as well, but the overall architecture typically follows the high-level model shown in Fig. 1.

Given the relatively uniform nature of the end-to-end IoT systems, it is not surprising that a large number of IoT platforms have emerged. According to IoT Analytics, in 2020 the number of known IoT platforms was 620[2]. In addition, there are a lot of company-specific IoT platform implementations that are less widely known.

Historically, IoT systems were very *cloud-centric* (Fig. 2) in the sense that nearly all the computation was performed in the cloud in a centralized fashion [6]. In contrast, the role of devices and gateways was limited mainly to sensor data aggregation, acquisition and actuation. However, as more computing power and storage has become available on the edge (devices and gateways), the more

---

[2] https://iot-analytics.com/iot-platform-companies-landscape-2020/.

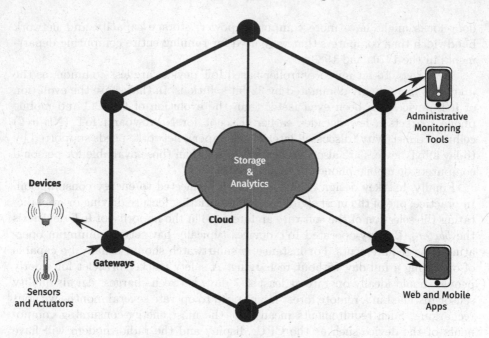

Fig. 2. Cloud-centric IoT architecture.

realistic it has become to perform significant computation also in IoT devices and gateways.

The recent development of the Internet of Things paradigm is enabled primarily by advances in hardware development. Hardware evolution has led to widespread availability of increasingly capable and power-efficient low-cost computing chips and development boards. These boards easily match or even exceed the memory and processing power capabilities that mobile phones or even PCs had in the late 1990s, and far surpass the processing capabilities of the early 8-bit and 16-bit personal computers from the early 1980s.

Examples of low-cost IoT development boards include the 10€ Arduino Nano Every (https://store.arduino.cc/arduino-nano-every) and the $4 Raspberry Pi Pico (https://www.raspberrypi.org/products/raspberry-pi-pico/). In spite of its low price, the latter device has computing capabilities that exceed those of the once dominant Intel 80386 and 80486 based personal computers in the late 1980s and early 1990s. Some of the more recently introduced devices, such as the popular $89 *Raspberry Pi 4B* and the $109 all-in-one keyboard-integrated Raspberry Pi 400 device have a quad-core ARM Cortex-A72 processor running at 1.5 GHz and 1.8 GHz, respectively – and are thus more powerful than many laptop computers only some 15 years ago.

The widespread availability of inexpensive IoT chips has made it possible to embed intelligence and Internet communication capabilities in virtually all everyday devices. Projecting five to ten years ahead, everyday objects in our surroundings such as coffee brewing machines, refrigerators, sauna stoves and door locks might have more computing power, storage capacity and network bandwidth than computers that were used for running entire computing departments in the 1970s and 1980s.

Nowadays, 16-bit microcontroller-based IoT devices are less common, as the market is increasingly dominated by 32-bit solutions. In that sense the evolution of IoT devices has been even faster than the evolution of the PC and mobile phone markets a few decades earlier. Except for Narrowband IoT (NB-IoT) cellular connectivity (discussed later in the paper), network speeds supported by today's IoT devices are also significantly faster than those available for personal computers or mobile phones in their early history.

Finally, IoT key design choices are often connected to energy consumption. In practice, one of the most significant differentiating feature driving or even dictating the selection of the software architecture in the majority of IoT devices is the *battery*. Battery-operated IoT devices typically have strict minimum operating time requirements. For instance, a smartwatch should usually be capable of operating a full day without recharging. A safety tracker bracelet for elderly people should ideally operate at least 4–7 days between charges. An air quality sensor installed in a remote forest might need to operate several months without recharging. Such requirements mean that the most energy-consuming components of the device such as the CPU, display and the radio modem will have to be chosen (and used) carefully to meet the power requirements. The form factor characteristics of the device (e.g., wearability and design aspects) play a significant role in determining the right tradeoffs, hence impacting also the type of software architecture that the device can support.

3   IoT Devices – Basic Software Architecture Options

Based on our experiences with various industrial IoT development efforts, the software architecture choices for IoT client devices can be classified as follows, ranging from simple to more complex architectures (Fig. 3 and Table 1):

Fig. 3. Example IoT devices for each architecture choice.

1. *No OS architecture*: for simplest sensing devices that do not need any operating system at all. Software is written specifically for the device, and software development is typically carried in-house. Hence, there is no need for third-party developer support, and support for firmware updates may be limited or non-existent. Given the fixed nature of software in these types of low-end

Table 1. Basic hardware configurations for IoT devices

Architecture choice	Typical device	Hardware	OS	RAM	Expected battery duration
No OS	Simple sensor devices (e.g., heartbeat sensor)	Low-end microcontrollers	None; basic drivers only	up to 10 kB	weeks-months
RTOS	More advanced sensors (e.g., feature watches)	Higher-end microcontrollers	Real-time OS (e.g., FreeRTOS, Nucleus, QNX)	10 KBs–1 MB	days-weeks
Language Runtime	Generic sensing solutions, "maker" devices	Off-the-shelf hardware	RTOS + VM supporting specific programming languages	100s kB to few MBs	days
Full OS	Generic sensing solutions, "maker" devices	Off-the-shelf hardware	Linux	1/2 to few MBs	N/A or days
App OS	High-end smartwatches	Off-the-shelf or custom hardware	Android Wear or Apple Watch OS	From 512 MB	up to 24 h
Server OS	Solutions benefiting from portable Web server	Off-the-shelf hardware	Linux and Node.js	10s of MBs	up to 24 h
Container OS	Solutions benefiting from fully isomorphic apps	Fully virtualized	Linux and Docker	GBs	N/A or hours

devices, the amount of RAM and Flash memory can be kept minimal. In many cases, only a few kilobytes or tens of kilobytes of RAM will suffice.

2. *RTOS architecture*: for more capable IoT devices that benefit from a real-time operating system. Several off-the-shelf systems exist, both commercial and open source. Software development for RTOS-based IoT devices is usually carried out in-house, since such devices do not typically provide any third-party developer APIs or the ability to reprogram the device dynamically (apart from performing a full firmware update). Memory requirements of RTOS-based architectures are comparable to No OS architectures, often necessitating as little as a few tens of kilobytes of RAM and a few hundred kilobytes of Flash memory. However, in recent years even in this area the amounts of memory have increased significantly; modern RTOS solutions may have megabytes of storage memory.

3. *Language runtime architecture*: for devices that require dynamic programming capabilities offered by languages such as Java, JavaScript or Python. Compared to No OS or RTOS solutions, language runtime based IoT devices are significantly more capable in the sense that they can support third-party application development and dynamic changes, i.e., updating the device software (or parts thereof) dynamically without having to reflash the entire firmware. The dynamic language runtime serves as the portable execution layer that enables third-party application development and the creation of developer-friendly application interfaces. Such capabilities leverage the interactive nature of the dynamic languages, allowing flexible interpretation and execution of code on the fly without compromising the security of the underlying execution environment and device.

Examples of IoT development boards that provide support for a *specific built-in language runtime or virtual machine (VM)* are: *Espruino* (https://www.espruino.com/) or *Tessel 2* (https://tessel.io/) which provide built-in support for JavaScript applications, while Pycom's *WiPy* boards (https://pycom.io/development-boards) enable Python development.

The technical capabilities and memory requirements of devices based on language runtime architecture vary considerably based on the supported language(s). Virtual machines for minimalistic programming languages such as Forth might require only a few tens of kilobytes of dynamic memory, while Java, JavaScript, WebAssembly, or Python VMs require at least several hundreds of kilobytes or preferably multiple megabytes of RAM. The size and complexity of the virtual machines also varies considerably, and thus the minimum amount of Flash or ROM memory can also range from a few hundreds of kilobytes to several megabytes.

4. *Full OS architecture*: for devices that are capable enough to host a full operating system (typically some variant of Linux). The presence of a full operating system brings a lot of benefits, such as built-in support for secure file transfers, user accounts, device management capabilities, security updates, very mature development toolchains, possibility to run third-party applications, and numerous other features. Compared to low-end No OS or RTOS architectures, the memory and CPU requirements of Full OS stacks are significantly higher. For instance, the desire to run a Linux-based operating system in a device bumps the RAM requirements from a few tens or hundreds of kilobytes (for an RTOS-based solution) up to half a megabyte at the minimum. Also, the significantly higher energy consumption requirements make it difficult to use such devices in use cases that require battery operation.

5. *App OS architecture*: for devices that are designed specifically to support third party application development. Located at the current high end of the IoT device spectrum, wearable device platforms such as Android Wear (https://www.android.com/wear/) or Apple watchOS (https://www.apple.com/watchos/) are in many ways comparable to mobile phone application platforms from 5–10 years ago. These wearable device platforms provide very rich platform capabilities and third-party developer APIs, but they also bump up the minimum hardware requirements considerably. For instance, already back in 2014, the minimum amount of RAM required by Android Wear was half a gigabyte (512 MB) – over 10,000 times more than the few tens of kilobytes of RAM required for simple IoT sensor devices. Furthermore, the processing power requirements of App OS devices are also dramatically higher than in simplest microcontroller-based IoT devices. Typically, an ARM Cortex-A class processor is mandated (for instance, an ARM A7 processor running at 1.2 GHz was stated as the minimum requirement for Android Wear back in 2014), limiting maximum battery duration to a few days, or only to a few hours in highly intensive use.

6. *Server OS architecture*: for devices that are capable enough to run a server-side operating system stack (typically Linux + Node.js). The Node.js ecosystem (https://nodejs.org/) has popularized the use of the JavaScript language also in server-side development, thus turning JavaScript into lingua franca for web development from client to cloud. By default, Node.js assumes the availability of at least 1.5 GB of RAM. However, Node.js can be configured

to operate with considerably smaller amounts of memory, starting from a few tens of megabytes. In addition to (or instead of) Node.js, there are several other web server offerings that are more tailored to embedded environments.

7. *Container OS architecture*: for high-end IoT devices that are powerful to host a virtualized, container-based operating system stack such as Docker or CoreOS Rocket (rkt). Given the independence of the physical execution environment that containers can provide, containers are a very attractive concept also for IoT development, especially in light of the technical diversity of IoT devices. Thus, although container technologies add considerable overhead compared to traditional binary software, their use has already started also in the context of IoT devices. From a purely technical viewpoint container-based architectures are definitely a viable option for IoT devices if adequate memory and other resources are available [7]. At the minimum, the host environment must typically have several gigabytes of RAM available, thus making this approach unsuitable for the vast majority of IoT devices.

4   Emergence of Edge IoT AI/ML Capabilities

One of the things unforeseen by our original taxonomy was the rapid emergence of AI/ML capabilities on the edge. These capabilities have made it possible to perform tasks such as object recognition, voice recognition, gesture detection and gas detection in IoT devices themselves. Only some five years ago, such tasks would have required significant data transfer and computation in the cloud.

In this section we will take a look at edge IoT AI/ML capabilities that have already resulted in significant changes in the future software architecture of IoT devices and their broader end-to-end system architecture.

From the viewpoint of IoT devices, current edge IoT AI/ML capabilities can be divided broadly into two or three categories based on whether AI/ML support is provided with dedicated hardware or in the form of software libraries. Software libraries can be further divided into generic libraries and such AI/ML libraries that have been provided to support specific sensors.

4.1   Dedicated AI/ML Hardware for the Edge

In the past few years, a broad variety of AI/ML enabled single board computers (SBCs) and modules have emerged, all providing remarkable edge processing capabilities at a reasonable price. Examples of such single board computers and modules include the following (in alphabetical order):

– *BeagleBone AI* (https://beagleboard.org/ai) – priced at about 115€ – is BeagleBoard.org's open source single-board computer (SBC) that is meant for use in home automation, industry automation and other commercial use cases. Beaglebone AI is intended for bridging the gap between small SBCs and more powerful industrial computers. The hardware and software of the BeagleBoard are fully open source.

- *Coral* (https://coral.ai/) is Google's product family for local, on-device AI applications. Google Coral product family consists of a number of standalone development boards, PC enhancement solutions (in the form factor of USB sticks or M.2 or PCIe accelerator boards), as well as modules that can be embedded into custom hardware products. Coral development boards such as the Dev Board Mini come pre-flashed with Mendel Linux, so the setup process only requires connecting to the board's shell console, updating some software, and then running a TensorFlow Lite model on the board. In contrast, the PC enhancement boards (such as the Coral Accelerator USB stick) can simply be plugged in to a host computer. After installing some additional TensorFlow-related software, the user can run typical examples such as object detection, pose detection, and keyphrase detection.
- *Khadas VIM3* (https://docs.khadas.com/vim3/) is an NPU (Neural Processing Unit) enabled development board that can be used as a standalone computer, small-footprint server or robotics system driver. Just like the other single-board AI/ML computers, Khadas VIM3 comes with a number of camera- and image-oriented sample applications for performing tasks such as object recognition.
- *NVIDIA Jetson* product family (https://www.nvidia.com/en-us/autonomous-machines/embedded-systems/). NVIDIA's Jetson product family provides a number of different options ranging from $59 Jetson Nano and $399 Jetson TX2 "supercomputer-on-a-module" all the way to Jetson AGX Xavier priced at $649 USD apiece. Each model is a complete System-on-Module (SOM) with CPU, GPU, PMIC (integrated power management), DRAM and flash storage. Jetson boards can run multiple neural networks in parallel for applications such as image classification, object detection, segmentation, and speech processing. Support for different AI/ML frameworks is provided. Even the smallest NVIDIA Jetson Nano model is rather powerful, featuring a quad core ARM Cortex A57 processor, 2 GB LPDDR4 memory, 16 GB eMMC Flash and NVIDIA Maxwell GPU with 128 cores. However, for more advanced video processing tasks, higher-level Jetson devices are recommended. The more powerful Jetson TX2 model features on-board AI support with an NVIDIA Pascal GPU, up to 8 GB of LPDDR4 memory, 59.7 GB/s of memory bandwidth, and a wide range of hardware interfaces. These devices are fit for various use cases, including also those that involve 'do-it-yourself' characteristics [8]. For software development, quite sophisticated tools are provided, including support for container-based deployment (https://docs.nvidia.com/egx/egx-introduction/).
- *ROCK Pi N10* (https://wiki.radxa.com/RockpiN10) – developed by Radxa – is an inexpensive NPU-equipped single-board computer that is part of the ROCK Pi product family (https://rockpi.org/). It is being offered in three variants: ROCK Pi N10 Model A, ROCK Pi N10 Model B and ROCK Pi N10 Model C. The only differences between these variants are the price, RAM and Storage capacities. The base variant of ROCK Pi N10 is available at $99, while its range topping variant comes in at $169. All the variants

are equipped with an NPU that offers up to 3 TOPS (Tera Operations Per Second) of performance.

For a summary of single-board computers for AI/ML applications, refer to: https://itsfoss.com/best-sbc-for-ai/

4.2 Software-Based AI/ML Solutions for the Edge

In addition to custom hardware, AI/ML capabilities can be added to edge devices also in the form of software libraries. As already indicated by the summary of emerging AI/ML hardware technologies above, AI/ML software is being redesigned to support intelligent operations away from the cloud. This involves the ability to feed local sensor data to pre-trained models running on the sensor devices themselves, or even to use such data to locally train or improve the training of such models, thus paving the way towards offline and disconnected operation of self-calibrating sensors.

Software-based AI/ML solutions can be divided into (a) generic solutions and (b) those that have been customized to support specific devices or sensors; we will discuss both categories below.

Generic Solutions. Popular generic AI/ML solutions include *TinyML* [9] which allows the integration of ML capabilities with microcontroller units for analytics applications which require an extremely low power (typically in the mW range and below). In addition, existing ML tools and libraries such as TensorFlow are being adapted so they can be used to perform ML inferences on such devices. Popular systems include *TensorFlow Lite* and *TensorFlow Lite for Microcontrollers*. Moreover, customized tools are needed for converting ML models trained on high-powered devices so that these models can be simplified to fit in low-power devices. Other libraries, e.g., the Artificial Intelligence for Embedded Systems (AIfES) library developed at Fraunhofer IMS, have been designed with the consideration of the limitations of small powered devices from the start. For example, they can ensure that pre-allocated, static data structures are used to store the weights and the training data of a neural network [10].

As an example of an inexpensive microcontroller that provides support for software-based AI/ML capabilities, we mention the *Arduino Nano 33 BLE Sense* (https://docs.arduino.cc/hardware/nano-33-ble-sense). This device is intended for developers who are becoming familiar with embedded machine learning; it combines multiple sensors for inertial measurements, digital microphone, temperature, humidity and barometric pressure, proximity, light and gesture recognition with the ability to run MicroPython code invoking the TensorFlow Lite libraries.

Custom Solutions for Specific Devices/Sensors. The main arguments in favor of using AI/ML capabilities on the edge include both the abundance of incoming data which can be locally classified or filtered as well as privacy concerns [11]. In the past year or so, new technologies have been announced that will provide such processing capabilities at the *very* edge – as part of the sensors that can be embedded in the IoT devices. A good example of such technology is the AI-enabled Bosch BME688 gas sensor (https://www.bosch-sensortec.com/products/environmental-sensors/gas-sensors/bme688/) that can be trained to detect different gas compositions. The sensor itself is very small – only 3 mm by 3 mm by 1 mm, and it costs under 10€ apiece. In practice, the AI/ML capabilities of this sensor are provided in the form of a custom library that needs to be compiled into the firmware of the microcontroller that is hosting the sensor.

5   Towards Seamless Device-Edge-Cloud Continuum

Historically, IoT systems were very cloud-centric, with the majority of computation taking place centrally in the cloud. However, given the rapidly increasing computing and storage capacities of IoT devices, it is clear that in the future IoT systems it can be very beneficial to balance and seamlessly transfer intelligence between the cloud and the edge. Such capabilities are important, since the ability to preprocess data in IoT devices allows for lower latencies and can also significantly reduce unnecessary data traffic between the devices and cloud. In general, in recent years there has been a noticeable trend towards *edge computing*, i.e., cloud computing systems that perform a significant part of their data processing at the edge of the network, near the source of the data [12]. In IoT systems supporting edge computing, devices and gateways play a key role in filtering and preprocessing the data, thus reducing the need to upload all the collected data to the cloud for further processing.

Intelligence at the Edge. The edge of a modern computing system consists of a broad range of devices such as base stations, smart phones, tablets, measurement and sensing devices, gateways, and so on. In contrast with the cloud, the computing capacity, memory and storage of edge devices are often limited. However, these devices are conveniently located near the endpoint, thus offering low latency. Due to limitations in connectivity and the increasing capacity of edge devices, intelligence in a modern end-to-end computing system is moving towards the edge, first to gateways and then to devices. This includes both generic software functions, and – more importantly – time critical AI/ML features for processing data available in the edge, referred to as Edge AI. It has been envisioned that evolution of telecom infrastructures beyond 5G will consider highly distributed AI, moving the intelligence from the central cloud to edge computing resources [13]. Furthermore, edge intelligence is a necessity for a world where intelligent autonomous systems are commonplace.

AI/ML can be a new reason for using heterogeneous technologies across the different types of devices, assuming that we accept each technology domain to remain separate, as indicated in the taxonomy presented in Sect. 3. In contrast, the emergence of AI/ML capabilities at the edge can also provide a motivation for technologies that blur the line between the cloud and the edge with approaches that scale AI/ML operations down to small devices (e.g., TensorFlow Lite, AIfES, TinyML) or provide seamless flexibility for the migration of components that host the AI/ML features (e.g., isomorphic and liquid software).

Isomorphic IoT Systems.   One of the key challenges for IoT system development is development complexity. As we have pointed out in our previous papers (see, e.g., [14]), the software technologies required for the development of key elements of an end-to-end IoT system – devices, gateways and cloud back-end – tend to be very diverse. For the development of cloud components, developers need to be familiar with technologies such as Docker, Kubernetes, NGINX, Grafana, Kibana, Node.js, and numerous Node.js libraries and modules. Gateways are commonly built upon native or containerized Linux or – in case of consumer solutions – on top of mobile operating systems such as Android or iOS. In contrast, IoT device development still requires the mastery of "classic" embedded software development skills and low-level programming languages such as C. In addition, IoT systems commonly include web-based user interfaces that are developed with frontend web technologies such as React.js or Angular. The palette of development technologies covered by the entire end-to-end system is so wide that hardly any developer can master the full spectrum.

Earlier in this paper, we noted that software containers and virtualization technologies are becoming available also in IoT devices. We predict that within the next five to ten years, this may lead the industry to *isomorphic IoT system architectures* [14] – in analogy to isomorphic web applications [15] – in which the devices, gateways and the cloud will have the ability to run *exactly the same software components and services*, allowing flexible migration of code between any element in the overall system. In an isomorphic system architecture, there does not have to be any significant technical differences between software that runs in the backend or in the edge of the network. Rather, when necessary, software can freely "roam" between the cloud and the edge in a seamless, liquid fashion. However, aiming at this goal means new research for lighter-weight containers [16] as well as new solutions for runtime migration [17].

Granted, there will still be various technical differences in the components that are intended for different elements in the end-to-end system. Still, it should be easier to constrain where isomorphic software can or cannot be deployed as opposed to rewriting it completely when the need for a new deployment arises. For instance, those components that are intended for interfacing with specific sensors or radio protocols in IoT devices do not necessarily have to run in end-user web or mobile applications. Conversely, end user UI components are not expected to run in IoT devices that do not have a display at all. However, the key point here is the reduced need to learn completely different development technologies and paradigms. This is important if we wish to reduce the intellectual burden and lower the steep learning curve that hampers end-to-end IoT systems development today.

In many ways, isomorphic architectures can be seen as the missing link in IoT development. Instead of having to learn and use many different incompatible ways of software development, in an isomorphic system architecture a small number of base technologies will suffice and will be able to cover different aspects of end-to-end development. At this point it is still difficult to predict which technologies will become dominant in this area. The earlier mentioned software container technologies such as *Docker* and *CoreOS rkt* are viable guesses, even though their memory and computing power requirements may seem ludicrous from the viewpoint of today's IoT devices. Amazon's *Greengrass* system (https://aws.amazon.com/greengrass/) also points out to a model in which the same programming model can be used both in the cloud and in IoT devices; in Greengrass, the programming platform is Amazon's Lambda. In the smaller end of the spectrum, the *Toit* system (https://toit.io/) developed by people from Google's original V8 JavaScript VM team seems very promising.

In our recent IEEE Computer paper [14], we predicted that isomorphic IoT systems would most likely form around two primary base technologies: (1) *JavaScript/ECMAScript* [18] and (2) *WebAssembly* [19]. The former is the *de facto* language for web applications both for the web browser and the cloud backend (Node.js); it is currently the most viable option for implementing static isomorphism, i.e., to allow the use of the same programming language throughout the end-to-end system. The latter is a binary instruction format to be executed on a stack-based virtual machine that can leverage contemporary hardware [20, 21]; we see WebAssembly as the best option for providing support for dynamic isomorphism, i.e., the ability to use of common runtime that is powerful but small enough to fit also in low-end IoT devices. Note that these options are not mutually exclusive, i.e., it would be possible to implement an architecture in which WebAssembly is used as the unifying runtime but in which JavaScript is used as the programming language throughout the end-to-end system.

Liquid Software. Liquid software [22], also known as cross-device experience roaming [23], is a concept where software can dynamically flow between different computers, basically allowing execution of code and associated user experiences to be transferred dynamically and seamlessly from one computational element to another. While the majority of the work associated with liquid software has focused on the UI layer (e.g., [24–26]), the concept is applicable to any situation in which software can be dynamically redeployed and adapted to take full advantage of the storage and computational resources provided by different devices that are shared by one or multiple collaborating users.

In essence, building liquid applications needs two facilities. One is the ability to relocate code flexibly across different computing entities, which is an elementary expectation and principle also for the isomorphism of software. The second facility is the ability to synchronize the state of the application and its UI across all devices running the code. This has been implemented by Apple in their Continuity/Handoff framework [27], which today is the most advanced industrial implementation, as well as by many academic agent frameworks (e.g., [28]) and web development frameworks (e.g., [29,30]).

Cellular IoT and Mesh Networking Technologies Will Increase the Role of Edge Computing. Another area in which there has been a lot of development after the creation of our initial software architecture taxonomy are radio technologies and communication protocols. These emerging technologies can have a significant impact on the overall IoT system architecture, thus also impacting the device-edge-cloud continuum. We focus especially on two categories: (1) LPWAN (Low-Power Wide Area Network) technologies and (2) local mesh networking connectivity.

Low-Power Wide Area Network Technologies. Low-power wide area network (LPWAN) technologies make it possible for IoT devices to communicate with the cloud directly from a distance – without the need for gateway devices in the middle. Prominent LPWAN technologies include Cellular IoT technologies such as NarrowBand-IoT and LTE-M, as well as more proprietary technologies such as LoRa (https://lora-alliance.org/) and SIGFOX (https://www.sigfox.com/). We do especially wish to highlight the 3GPP Cellular IoT radio technologies – NB-IoT and LTE-M – which make it possible to connect virtually any artifact directly to the Internet at low cost and minimal battery consumption. Cellular IoT technologies can eliminate (or at least dramatically reduce the need for) gateways in IoT systems, allowing IoT devices to communicate with the cloud directly.

Standardization of 3GPP Cellular IoT technologies was completed in 2016, and these technologies have already been widely deployed onto existing commercial cellular networks. In fact, nationwide Cellular IoT coverage for IoT devices is already available in numerous countries, although these capabilities are still in relatively low use. Chipsets and hardware modules supporting Cellular IoT technologies are available from various vendors, including Gemalto, Nordic Semiconductor, Quectel, Sierra Wireless and u-Blox.

Local Mesh Networking Connectivity. Another area that is likely to have a significant impact on the overall topology of IoT systems is peer-to-peer (P2P) connectivity between IoT devices. New technologies such as *Bluetooth Mesh* (https://www.bluetooth.com/specifications/mesh-specifications) are making it feasible for IoT devices to exchange information with each other efficiently with minimal latencies – thus further reducing the need for more expensive communication with the cloud. As opposed to current cloud-centric IoT systems, P2P and edge computing are fundamental characteristics of systems in which low latency is required. An interesting broader question is whether there will still be need for "constrained" protocols such as CoAP or MQTT, or will the landscape be dominated by broader *de facto* standard solutions such as REST/HTTPS. At the time of this writing, MQTT (https://mqtt.org/) seems to be the dominant IoT system communication protocol, although there are emerging standards such as Matter (https://buildwithmatter.com/) that may replace it in the longer run.

Even though the dominant LPWAN and mesh networking protocols have not been fully established yet, together the emergence of mesh networking and LPWAN technologies can be expected to *lead to a drastically increased role of edge computing*, as well as to a significantly reduced role of gateways in the overall IoT system architecture. As the role of the gateways withers down, IoT devices themselves will take a more active role in the overall E2E architecture.

Table 2. High-level comparison of software architecture options

Feature	No OS/RTOS	Language VM	Full OS	App OS	Server OS	Container OS
Typical development language	C or assembly	Java, JavaScript, Python	C or C++	Java, Objective-C, Swift	JavaScript	Various
Libraries	None or System-specific	Language-specific generic libraries	OS libraries, generic UI libraries	Platform libraries	Node.js NPM modules	Various
Dynamic SW updates	Firmware updates only (Reflashing)	Yes	Yes	Yes (App Stores)	Yes	Yes (Image Snapshots)
Third-party apps supported	No	Yes	Yes	Yes (Rich APIs)	Yes	Yes
AI/ML at the edge	Emerging	Yes	Yes	Yes	Yes	Yes
Isomorphic apps possible	No	Yes	Only if the same OS/HW	Yes	Yes	Yes

6   Wrapping Things Up

In summary, there exists a broad range of software architecture options and stacks for IoT devices, depending on the expected usage, power budget, and memory requirements (see Table 1 earlier in the paper) and the need to support dynamic software deployment and/or third-party development as well as intelligent decision making on the device. Table 2 provides a condensed summary of the software architecture options for IoT devices, focusing on the broader architectural implications in the device-edge-cloud continuum. It should be noted that the options summarized in the table are by no means exclusive. For instance, as already mentioned above, devices based on the language runtime architecture commonly have an RTOS underneath. Likewise, in Full OS platforms, it is obviously possible to run various types of language runtimes and virtual machines as long as an adequate amount of memory is available to host those runtime(s). In general, the more capable the underlying execution environment is, the more feasible it is to run various types of software architectures, platforms and applications on it.

7   Conclusions

In this paper we have revisited a taxonomy of software architecture options for IoT devices, starting from the most limited sensing devices to high-end devices featuring full-fledged operating systems and developer frameworks. After examining each of the basic options, we presented a comparison and some broader observations, followed by relevant emerging trends and future directions. In particular, we noted that the emergence of inexpensive AI/ML hardware – unforeseen by our original taxonomy – is increasing the role of the edge in IoT systems. Later in the paper, we additionally predicted that new communication technologies such as Cellular IoT and mesh networking will alter the overall topology of IoT systems quite considerably, e.g., leading to a reduced role of gateways in the overall architecture.

Although the vast majority of IoT devices today have fairly simple software stacks, the overall software stack complexity can be expected to increase due to hardware evolution and the general desire to support edge computing, AI/ML technologies and software containers. In light of these observations, we made a case for isomorphic IoT systems in which development complexity is alleviated with consistent use of technologies across the entire end-to-end system, providing a more seamless technology continuum from IoT devices on the edge all the way to the cloud. In such systems, different subsystems and computational entities can be programmed with a consistent set of technologies. Although fully isomorphic IoT systems are still some years away, their arrival may ultimately dilute or even dissolve the boundaries between the cloud and its edge, allowing computations to be performed in those elements that provide the optimal tradeoff between performance, storage, network speed, latency and energy efficiency. We hope that this paper, for its part, encourages people to investigate these exciting new directions in more detail.

References

1. Wasik, B.: In the Programmable World. All Our Objects Will Act as One, Wired, May 2013
2. Munjin, D., Morin, J.H.: Toward Internet of Things application markets. In: 2012 IEEE International Conference on Green Computing and Communications (Green-Com), pp. 156–162. IEEE (2012)
3. Taivalsaari, A., Mikkonen, T.: Roadmap to the programmable world: software challenges in the IoT era. IEEE Softw. 34(1), 72–80 (2017)
4. Taivalsaari, A., Mikkonen, T.: Beyond the next 700 IoT platforms. In: Proceedings of 2017 IEEE International Conference on Systems, Man and Cybernetics (SMC 2017, Banff, Canada, 5–8 October), pp. 3529–3534 (2017)
5. Taivalsaari, A., Mikkonen, T.: On the development of IoT systems. In: Proceedings of the 3rd IEEE International Conference on Fog and Mobile Edge Computing (FMEC 2018, Barcelona, Spain, 23–26 April 2018) (2018)
6. Botta, A., De Donato, W., Persico, V., Pescapé, A.: Integration of cloud computing and Internet of Things: a survey. Future Gener. Comput. Syst. 56, 684–700 (2016)
7. Celesti, A., Mulfari, D., Fazio, M., Villari, M., Puliafito, A.: Exploring container virtualization in IoT clouds. In: 2016 IEEE International Conference on Smart Computing, pp. 1–6. IEEE (2016)
8. Cass, S.: Nvidia makes it easy to embed AI: the Jetson nano packs a lot of machine-learning power into DIY projects. IEEE Spectr. 57(7), 14–16 (2020)
9. Sanchez-Iborra, R., Skarmeta, A.F.: TinyML-Enabled frugal smart objects: challenges and opportunities. IEEE Circuits Syst. Mag. 20(3), 4–18 (2020)
10. Gembaczka, P., Heidemann, B., Bennertz, B., Groeting, W., Norgall, T., Seidl, K.: Combination of sensor-embedded and secure server-distributed artificial intelligence for healthcare applications. Curr. Dir. Biomed. Eng. 5(1), 29–32 (2019)
11. Greengard, S.: AI on edge. Commun. ACM 63(9), 18–20 (2020)
12. Shi, W., Dustdar, S.: The promise of edge computing. IEEE Comput. 49(5), 78–81 (2016)
13. Peltonen, E., et al.: 6G White Paper on Edge Intelligence. arXiv preprint arXiv:2004.14850 (2020)

14. Mikkonen, T., Pautasso, C., Taivalsaari, A.: Isomorphic Internet of Things architectures with web technologies. Computer **54**, 69–78 (2021)
15. Strimpel, J., Najim, M.: Building Isomorphic JavaScript Apps: From Concept to Implementation to Real-World Solutions. O'Reilly Media Inc., Newton (2016)
16. Park, M., Bhardwaj, K., Gavrilovska, A.: Toward lighter containers for the edge. In: 3rd USENIX Workshop on Hot Topics in Edge Computing (HotEdge 20) (2020)
17. Fuggetta, A., Picco, G.P., Vigna, G.: Understanding code mobility. IEEE Trans. Softw. Eng. **24**(5), 342–361 (1998)
18. ECMA International: Standard ECMA-262: ECMAScript 2020 Language Specification, June 2020. https://www.ecma-international.org/publications/standards/Ecma-262.html
19. World Wide Web Consortium: WebAssembly Core Specification (2019). https://webassembly.github.io/spec/core/_download/WebAssembly.pdf
20. Bryant, D.: WebAssembly outside the browser: a new foundation for pervasive computing. In: Keynote at ICWE 2020, 9–12 June 2020, Helsinki, Finland (2020)
21. Jacobsson, M., Willén, J.: Virtual machine execution for wearables based on WebAssembly. In: Sugimoto, C., Farhadi, H., Hämäläinen, M. (eds.) BODYNETS 2018. EICC, pp. 381–389. Springer, Cham (2020). https://doi.org/10.1007/978-3-030-29897-5_33
22. Taivalsaari, A., Mikkonen, T., Systä, K.: Liquid software manifesto: the era of multiple device ownership and its implications for software architecture. In: 38th Annual IEEE Computer Software and Applications Conference (COMPSAC), pp. 338–343. IEEE (2014)
23. Brudy, F., et al.: Cross-Device taxonomy: survey, opportunities and challenges of interactions spanning across multiple devices. In: Proceedings of the 2019 CHI Conference on Human Factors in Computing Systems, pp. 1–28 (2019)
24. Voutilainen, J.-P., Mikkonen, T., Systä, K.: Synchronizing application state using virtual DOM trees. In: Casteleyn, S., Dolog, P., Pautasso, C. (eds.) ICWE 2016. LNCS, vol. 9881, pp. 142–154. Springer, Cham (2016). https://doi.org/10.1007/978-3-319-46963-8_12
25. Gallidabino, A., Pautasso, C.: The Liquid.js framework for migrating and cloning stateful web components across multiple devices. In: Proceedings of the 25th International Conference Companion on World Wide Web, pp. 183–186 (2016)
26. Husmann, M., Rossi, N.M., Norrie, M.C.: Usage analysis of cross-device web applications. In: Proceedings of the 5th ACM International Symposium on Pervasive Displays, pp. 212–219 (2016)
27. Gruman, G.: Apple's Handoff: What Works, and What Doesn't. InfoWorld, San Francisco (2014)
28. Systä, K., Mikkonen, T., Järvenpää, L.: HTML5 agents: mobile agents for the web. In: Krempels, K.-H., Stocker, A. (eds.) WEBIST 2013. LNBIP, vol. 189, pp. 53–67. Springer, Heidelberg (2014). https://doi.org/10.1007/978-3-662-44300-2_4
29. Gallidabino, A., Pautasso, C.: Decentralized computation offloading on the edge with liquid WebWorkers. In: Mikkonen, T., Klamma, R., Hernández, J. (eds.) ICWE 2018. LNCS, vol. 10845, pp. 145–161. Springer, Cham (2018). https://doi.org/10.1007/978-3-319-91662-0_11
30. Gallidabino, A., Pautasso, C.: Multi-Device complementary view adaptation with liquid media queries. J. Web Eng. **18**(8), 761–800 (2020)

Author Index

Printed in the United States
by Baker & Taylor Publisher Services

Printed in the United States
by Baker & Taylor Publisher Services